NOVEMBER/DECEMBER

FOREWORD
by the Vicar of St Martin-in-the-Fields

Just inside St Martin-in-the-Fields there is a prayer board. People come and leave notes on it. Some are addressed direct to God. Others ask us to pray for people and things. Either way this church is known to be a place of prayer. On the hundreds of slips of paper pinned each week to this board, people bring themselves and those for whom they care to God. It is one of the most natural things in the world to do.

I grew up at a time when clergy tended to say that prayer is difficult. It isn't. Living out the implications of our prayers can be difficult but prayer itself is as simple as breathing. It is one of our life instincts, a response to the wonder and complexity of God's creation. Jesus taught us to pray for what we want and the very process of praying, of voicing our wants, deepens the relationship and refines what we really want from God, for ourselves and others. As with so much else in life, we learn to pray by doing it and by being with others who do it well.

Some prayer is a solitary, silent occupation. There is no short cut to a life lived with God except by putting in the hours and by trying to pray, however inadequately, in the presence of God. I am grateful for the many people who are St Martin-in-the-Fields and who pray privately and faithfully day by day. There are also more than twenty services every week in the church. Come on a Sunday and you may find several hundred people present at a service. At others, especially mid-week, there will be only a tiny handful of people. These services are the heartbeat of the church: they oxygenate the blood and keep us alive to God's presence among us.

At St Martin's lay members take turns to lead our prayers on weekday evenings and at our main service on Sunday mornings. People take an enormous amount of trouble to prepare these intercessions, prayers to God spoken by an individual for the whole community. Sometimes these prayers are crafted by a wordsmith who has polished every phrase. At other times there is the rawness and passion of the less articulate but deeply felt. The prayers that gather us best as a

CONTENTS

MAY/JUNE

JULY/AUGUST

SEPTEMBER/OCTOBER

THE NAKED YEAR

prayers from the heart of London

Douglas Board

As with any other form of intimacy, the vital ingredients of prayer are honesty and an openness to being touched. This book of original prayers and reflections brings these qualities to such varied themes as sexuality, racism, humour, freedom, music, poverty and violence – as well as the Christian understanding of death and resurrection. Arranged around dates from 1 January to 31 December, these prayers will engage powerfully those with little familiarity with the Christian year, as well as energising and inspiring many who know it well.

'These prayers do not reflect the cloister but show what it is to pray in the eye of the storm, aware of the lovelessness of a world on the edge. They are an exercise in practical divinity which should stimulate us to build up our own personal calendars of prayer.'

Rt Revd and Rt Hon Richard Chartres,
Bishop of London

St Martin-in-the-Fields Ltd

© 2004 Douglas Board
The Naked Year ~ prayers from the heart of London

ISBN 1-871587-01-8

Published by:
St Martin-in-the-Fields Ltd
Trafalgar Square
London WC2N 4JJ
www.smitf.org

The right of Douglas Board to be identified as author of
this work has been asserted by him in accordance with the
Copyright, Designs and Patents Act 1988.

A CIP catalogue record for this book is available from the
British Library.

Design & production co-ordinated by:
The Better Book Company Ltd
Havant
Hampshire PO9 2XH

Printed in England.

Cover photograph: *Ecce homo (behold the man)!*
Mark Wallinger's life-size sculpture of Jesus in Trafalgar Square around
the turn of the millennium. The low winter sunshine also picks out St
Martin-in-the-Fields Church in the background. The sculpture was
unveiled on 21 July 1999, the first of a series of innovative exhibits
on the Square's 'fourth plinth'.
Photograph by Tricia Sibbons.

community are the ones that feel "real", where people have brought the world into the church to do serious business with God.

This book of prayers by Douglas Board has part of its genesis in his leading the public prayer of St Martin-in-the-Fields. Douglas is committed to an intelligent and imaginative Christianity, using the gifts God has given him in worship as well as he does in the rest of his life and work. More than most he is committed to engaging the liturgy in church with his experience of daily life. He has had the courage to do his best in voicing public prayer with and for us without pretending that he already knows the answer straight from God.

If the process of prayer is a "stripping down" of ourselves so that we can be open to God, so in *The Naked Year* there is a sense of us standing as a Christian community vulnerable before God. This is the pattern of God in Jesus. It is vividly illustrated in Trafalgar Square at the turn of the Millennium by Mark Wallinger's statue *Ecce Homo* photographed on the cover of this book. In the monumental space of Trafalgar Square which celebrates the great achievements of national heroes, the life-size figure of "the man" Christ inverts the powers of this world and from the corner of the Square catches our attention.

This is the experience of a church "in the fields" in the heart of London. It is paradoxical and playful, searching and centred on the God we know in Jesus Christ. *The Naked Year* is among the best we can offer from the life of this church. I hope it will help you to pray as it has helped Douglas and us.

Revd Nicholas Holtam

St Martin-in-the-Fields exists to honour God, and to enable questioning, open-minded people to discover for themselves the significance of Jesus Christ.

ABOUT PRAYER

What is prayer?

One of the least noted insights into prayer to emerge during the twentieth century occurs early in that marvellous film *A Fish Called Wanda* (screenplay by John Cleese). The scene is the large garden of an English house in sunshine. Birds are singing. A dog barks. Archie, a barrister, walks across from the house towards his wife Wendy, who is sitting in a garden chair reading a magazine. She does not look up.

ARCHIE *Hello Wendy! Had a good day?*

WENDY *(in unbroken flow) I spent the morning trying to get the waste disposal man to come, had lunch with Marjorie Brooks who takes up the entire meal complaining about her husband and then I had to play three rubbers with Philippa Hunter and I come back here and Sandersons have sent the wrong flowers.*

ARCHIE *Oh no. (pause) Would you like some tea?*

WENDY *(unappeased) Yes!*

ARCHIE *I won the case.*

WENDY *This is the first moment I've had to myself all day.*

ARCHIE *(in the kitchen, to his daughter in riding gear) Hello, Portia, how was the show?*

PORTIA *Awful daddy. I've got to have a new horse.*

ARCHIE *But I thought you liked Phantom.*

PORTIA   *He's not fit for dog meat. Can I change him please dad? It's*
          absolutely vital and it won't cost much.

WENDY   *Aren't you making the tea Archie? I suppose I'd better do it.*

ARCHIE   *No, no, let me do it.*

WENDY   *(emphatically, with irritation) No I'll do it.*

Too often prayer belongs to one of the two overworked traditions
exemplified in this script: we subject God to a flow of news reports
(Wendy) or of demands (Portia) uninterrupted by any tangible
sense of the presence of an Other. Archie has won the case, but no
one is listening. In the garden and then in the kitchen, there is no
intimacy.

In another garden, there was once intimacy with God. 'And the
man and his wife were both naked, and were not ashamed … They
heard the sound of the Lord God walking in the garden at the
time of the evening breeze' (Genesis 2: 25, 3: 8). The premise of
this book is the Christian teaching that this intimacy which God
made us to desire and to enjoy, which was lost, is available to us
now. We may no longer be in the Garden of Eden. We may be in
Trafalgar Square, or pressed together in the Tube underneath it. But
wherever we are, God can walk and talk with us, and we with God,
naked and without pretence. That, I believe, is prayer. God longs to
meet us there.

Formal or informal, long or short, orchestrated or sparse, daring
or restrained – prayer is not necessarily one of these or another,
any more than music is. The prayers and reflections in this book
vary in style. There is a universe of other styles besides – notably
silence. One is not better than another. The relevant question is,
on different occasions what words, thoughts or feelings express
compellingly who we are and who we are with. It is the *being-with*
that makes them prayers.

ABOUT THIS YEAR

This book is a series of dates. In one sense, it is exactly that – a series of forty-two dates, progressing through a year from January to December. Some of the dates are fixed, like New Year's Day (1 January) or the destruction of the World Trade Center (11 September). Others are seasonally fixed, like Easter (occurring at spring time but varying in calendar date with the cycles of the moon around the Earth). Yet others are unfixed, depending upon events in our own lives, such as weddings or commitment ceremonies and funerals. Arbitrarily this book places weddings in August and funerals in November but any other placings would be as valid.

But this book is also a series of "dates" with God in the other sense. If prayer is about intimacy, what God is revealed within the Christian tradition? Do I want to be intimate with him (or her)? We are long past any era in Britain in which the answers to those questions could be taken for granted. We need to get to know each other and each other's worlds, if indeed we are to stand together naked and without pretence. So, God, your place or mine?

For God the original, the infinite and the ultimate, of course that question is meaningless. Not so for God expressed through institutional Christianity; he definitely appears to have "his" place, expressed in the Bible, liturgies, creeds and other language which is not naturally mine. He has his calendar (Epiphany, for example) and I have mine.

So the dates in this book have two sources. The dates "at his place" are some of the principal events and festivals marked in the Christian year. The dates "at mine" are chosen to reflect major themes of life as I see and experience it lived around me, in London (symbolised by Trafalgar Square) at the start of this century. Any such choices must be idiosyncratic and incomplete. Mine include friendship, family, freedom, love, sexuality, racism, humour,

music and death (for others see the Index of Subjects and Themes).
Where the dates chosen revolve around people, the people are not
all Christian or virtuous. Simply, the themes which they bring to
life are – naked and without pretence – parts of my world through
which I need to walk with God, evening breeze or no evening
breeze, if we are to get to know each other better.

The dates may have two sources, but of course ultimately only one
root, since God is the God who made me, and Trafalgar Square and
everything in it.

About half of these prayers have been prayed over a number of
years in services at St Martin-in-the-Fields Church, in Trafalgar
Square. In a few cases the date when the prayers were used is given,
if this adds context. In so far as there is good in this material it
is the product of twenty-five years of teaching, worship, prayer
and nurturing by this Church of England community. In so far
as there is misjudgement or error, no one is accountable but me.
Quotations are identified as such in the text with sources set out
under Acknowledgements and Sources, which also lists texts which
provided important factual background.

To Tricia

NEW YEAR'S DAY

(1 January)

Great Britain has only celebrated New Year's Day on 1 January since 1752 (twenty-six years after the present St Martin-in-the-Fields Church was completed). With or without a sore head, it is pre-eminently a day for looking forward.

Tomorrow, God, as we rise together
As we eat together
As we meet other people
As we tire together
As we collapse together
You who made this house of my being and share it with me
You will still stand at the door and knock.

All day long
Let me open and re-open the door of my house
Making a reply which needs no words.

So may all our tomorrows gradually become one unbroken prayer
In which our silences and our words are equally aflame
With the intimate communication of lovers.

In Jesus' name we ask.

EPIPHANY

(6 January)

Epiphany is the Christian festival which marks the revelation of the newly-born Jesus to the magi or wise men, led from the East by a star.

In our extraordinarily individualistic society, why are almost all of us happy to use as our most personal name something which others gave us, in whose choosing we had no part? This is hardly to be explained by arguing that names are unimportant to us.

Perhaps we accept to such a large degree our names as given because our identities, which our names signify, are an important measure also given. We do not, at least in any logical or unfettered way, decide who we shall be; rather we discover ourselves. We participate in our own creation, but from raw material which we are given. But what is this process of discovery? What is it about "I" which *is* I?

A growing child sits unwrapping a present. In this solitary version of the children's game "pass the parcel", the present has many layers of wrapping paper. Each layer represents a period of time, perhaps a year; and in between each layer is a surprise – experiences, abilities, setbacks. We watch the child growing older before our eyes. We think first that the child is meant to play with the surprises only briefly, and keep unwrapping the far more valuable real present. What if one of the surprises is too captivating and the child discards the real present? But as the child ages, a different perspective strikes us. What if – devoted monk-like to the task, with untouched toys piled around – the ageing child ultimately finds the parcel to be empty?

In becoming ourselves we decide, however slowly and awkwardly, what to keep and what to discard. For example, in the unwrapping of John Lennon, the child given this identity discovered both a lyrical and a musical talent, and a vicious appetite for making fun of people with disabilities or deformities through drawings, song and mimicry. One gift the adult kept, the other he tried to discard, as he similarly worked to discard violence which was quite deeply ingrained within him: 'I fought men and I hit women. That is why I am always on about peace ... I am a violent man who has learned not to be violent and to regret his violence' (quoted by Ray Coleman, p 557).

Epiphany is the unwrapping of a mystery. Traditionally at Epiphany we think of the unwrapping of the identity of Jesus in a manger and the revelation of his true identity as a king. Moreover a king whose kingdom would extend to all people – for the wise men who arrive by divine navigation and bearing gifts are not Jews like Jesus, but "from the East".

(Matthew 2: 9-11)

'and there, ahead of them, went the star that they had seen at its rising, until it stopped over the place where the child was. When they saw that the star had stopped, they were overwhelmed with joy. On entering the house they saw the child with Mary his mother, and they knelt down and paid him homage. Then opening their treasure-chests, they offered him gifts of gold, frankincense and myrrh.'

We are born; we are given a name; we are given family, or the absence of family; we are given circumstances, abilities, health, confidence, wealth or the absence of these things. With the insights of psychology, we realise that one person's gift is another person's baggage. We can see in the magi story all sorts of baggage – other people's baggage – being deposited in Jesus' nursery, just as it was in our own. (Whose is this stuff? And who asked them to give it to *me*?)

What can be most clearly identified as "you" or "I" is not the totality of what we are now or what we were given then, but the difference between the two: what we choose to do with what we are given; as we unwrap the present, what we accept and what we discard.

The baggage for Jesus includes an asserted kingship over you and me. The identity of Jesus lies in what he does with this. The assertion of the Christian faith is that to receive fully our own identity, we need to unwrap not only our own present, but his.

Almighty God
Even by your outrageous standards
This feels like the journey of a fool.
Still lead me on
And let us see if we can find this thing
Of which so much has been spoken:
My forgiven soul.

In Jesus' name I ask.

THE BIRTH OF MARTIN LUTHER KING

(15 January)

AND THE WEEK OF PRAYER FOR CHRISTIAN UNITY

The prayers which follow this introduction, which were prayed at St Martin-in-the-Fields on 20 January 2002, are framed in the Church of England tradition.

Martin Luther King Jr, born 15 January 1929 and assassinated in 1968 aged thirty-nine, is widely recognized as a giant in black history and American history. He was the first black American to be honoured with a public holiday (which falls, as does the annual week of prayer for Christian unity, at this time). Millions know of his speech on a sweltering Washington day in August 1963, when he said, 'I have a dream.'

But King's significance for the institutional churches has been less noticed. He – a third generation Baptist preacher – was adamant that the Church of God was in desperate need of reform, no less than the society in which it sat. He denounced division within the Church as vigorously as he denounced racism. Do we Christians remember the *religious* content in King's closing words that August, when he exhorted the 250,000 crowd to bring closer the day when 'all of God's children, black and white, *Jews and Gentiles, Protestants and Catholics,* will be able to join hands and sing in the words of the old spiritual – Free at last! Free at last! Thank God Almighty, we are free at last!'?

King lived and died for his belief that ordinary people would one day rise up in righteous non-violent judgement, to tell the powers that be that they would tolerate scandalous division no longer. In the Church of God, are we listening?

In this special week of prayer, we pray with urgency for the unity, humility and energy of your Church throughout the world.

On our knees before you with Elizabeth our Queen; on our knees before you with Rowan our archbishop; on our knees before you with Richard our bishop; we repent of all institutional pride in the Church of England which disfigures your glory.

This week we also give thanks for your servant and martyr Martin Luther King, whose dream was of the promised land of unity: the unity of all your children, black and white, Jew and Gentile, Protestant and Catholic. We remember his haunting words on the evening before his assassination:
'It really doesn't matter with me now. Because I've been to the mountain top … I've looked over and I've seen the Promised Land. I may not get there with you, but I want you to know tonight, that we as a people will get to the Promised Land.'

Open our eyes Lord, that we may see today and every day your promised land of unity. Every valley will be exalted; every hill and mountain shall be made low; your glory shall be revealed, and all flesh shall see it – together.

HOMELESSNESS SUNDAY

(last Sunday in January)

Homelessness Sunday is marked by a number of churches and charities on or around the last Sunday in January.

One disfiguring aspect of homelessness is not being treated as a person. Art is one way through which the individuality of people who are homeless can be expressed and honoured. This is the first of two poems included by permission in this book which were produced by the creative writing group at St Martin-in-the-Fields. The group works with people who are homeless in central London. The poems, which are not religious, have been chosen for two reasons. They allow someone who was (maybe is) homeless to speak in his own voice. And they paint their own picture of London life today.

This poem comes from *Orange for Farewells*: Writing from St Martin-in-the-Fields 2002.

THE GHETTO IN THE VENUE

I live in a drab part of London
near a small industrial estate
There's a pub nearby with a venue built on
It's called the Bull and Gate.

Aspiring rock bands play there
they're angry and dangerous and cool
They're always white and male and middle-class
and they've just left public school.

I'll tell you why I don't like Mondays
'cos they unload speakers, mike stands and keyboards and miles of
wire

---

from a big van hogging the pavement.
It's always a white one – on bloody hire.

But they're polite young men.
I explain to my African friend
who owns the nearby shop
that the colonisation of our pavement
is an essential part of Brit-Pop.

He seems to get my irony
and acknowledges it with a smile.
There's ten yards between us and the rockers.
Could as well be ten thousand miles.

I glance around at the natural scenery:
Hindu off-licence, Kurdish kebab shop and Greek Cypriot chippie
blend in this unselfconscious corner of the inner city.

But the bands of yoof-ful followers
stand out in their search for authenticity
uniforms adhere to what pressures from peers
says is non-conformity.

Woolly hats cling over the ears
Jeans whose crotch hangs down to the ground
The plumage, the postures of the pseudo drop-outs
who've dropped in to sample the post-grunge sound.

Milling around the venue's private entrance
They sip bottled designer beers.
In the pub itself Irish builders drink Guinness.
There's five seconds between them
Could as well be five thousand years.

Quentin Bile

The Naked Year

Lord Jesus Christ
You did not mock our symbols of identity. You did not despise the hands, the clothes, the smells and the accents which mark out a fisherman, a prostitute, a landlord or a teacher. But you always challenged us to reach beyond these symbols, and to realise that the only chasms between people are the ones within our hearts.
You never made a fisherman who was only a fisherman.
You never made a homeless person who was only homeless.
You never made a commuter hurrying by, or a shopper, a police officer or a bully who was only a commuter, a shopper, a police officer or a bully.
You only made children of God.
By your grace give us eyes which can see this.

THE PRESENTATION OF
CHRIST IN THE TEMPLE

(2 February)

Luke 2: 27-33, 36-38
Guided by the Spirit, Simeon came into the temple; and when the parents
brought in the child Jesus, to do for him what was customary under the law,
Simeon took him in his arms and praised God, saying, 'Master, now you are
dismissing your servant in peace, according to your word; for my eyes have
seen your salvation, which you have prepared in the presence of all peoples, a
light for revelation to the Gentiles and for glory to your people Israel.' And the
child's father and mother were amazed at what was being said about him.
There was also a prophet, Anna the daughter of Phanuel, of the tribe of Asher.
She was of a great age, having lived with her husband for seven years after her
marriage, then as a widow to the age of eighty-four. She never left the temple
but worshipped there with fasting and prayer night and day. At that moment
she came, and began to praise God and to speak about the child to all who
were looking for the redemption of Jerusalem.

This account of the fulfilment of Jewish religious observance lays
two points open to immediate view, namely that Jesus is a Jew and
that his relevance will be to all peoples – Jews and Gentiles (non-
Jews). These are truths central to Jesus' ministry. But if we glance to
the side of the scene, we notice that one of the participants is Joseph,
Jesus' father. There is an ambivalence in the gospels about Joseph; an
ambivalence which can connect with fathers, present and absent, today.

The airbrushing of politicians into and out of photographs of the
former Soviet regime became internationally notorious. One day
you were reviewing the May Day parade and taking the salute, then
in a later photograph of the same day you weren't. That pattern is
slightly reminiscent of the appearance and non-appearance of Joseph
in the gospels.

On the one hand, Joseph is carefully written into the two genealogies of Jesus (Matthew 1: 16, Luke 3: 23). On the other hand, his disappearance shortly thereafter from these two gospels and his near non-existence in the other two is stark. Mark is particularly brutal: no mention of any of Jesus' family until 3: 21 ('his family') – which gets spelled out a few verses later as 'Whoever does the will of God is my brother and sister and mother' (Mark 3: 35).

The point bears making more strongly. Mary, the mother of Jesus, receives a hymn of praise ('My soul magnifies the Lord', Luke 1: 46-55) which is sung in churches to this day. Zechariah, the father of John the Baptist, gets similar treatment ('Blessed be the Lord God of Israel', Luke 1: 68-79). Even Simeon – whom in ordinary language one might describe as a religious nutter hanging around the temple – gets his own song (above), said and sung in churches *daily* 2,000 years later.

But Joseph? Nothing – although his obedience to the angels of God in Matthew chapters 1 and 2 might reasonably have attracted a verse or two. In reality, he is a father whose presence and absence are equally problematic. The gospel writers can't live with him and they can't live without him. That modern idiom describes a modern ambivalence. Not all of us are sure what fathers are for – how they should be when they are present, and what is missing when they are absent.

Often when the gospel-writers include Joseph (for example in the genealogies) the writers seem to be making a noisy point about his presence. Similarly when absent (for example in Mark), the noise of a point being made may be equally loud. From this point of view the presentation of Christ in the temple is rather precious. It is a gospel scene in which we can be sure Joseph is present, but not in so important a way as to attract the airbrushers' attention. Can we catch something of the real Joseph from the unwitting side glances in Luke's picture? The account tells us that Simeon 'took [the infant Jesus] in his arms'. Picture it: Simeon, an old man, with thin, wiry arms. I find then that I also picture the infant Jesus in Joseph's arms, moments before Simeon arrives. For if it was unusual or unnatural for Joseph to hold his own child, what chance would there have been of his mother giving the baby to an unknown male? Moreover, the ceremony described is gender-specific – the presentation of every first-born Jewish male to the Lord.

So we are within striking distance of the text if we picture what does not otherwise appear in it, namely the young Joseph – a muscular, protective Joseph – the Joseph who left with his wife and new-born child by night for Egypt, and when it was safe brought them back again – the obedient and uncelebrated Joseph – presenting Jesus in the temple. Hold them there, the boy and his dad; a dad soon afterwards written out of accounts of his son's life.

When we portray God one-sidedly as "Father" we are right to be conscious of the excluding effect of that portrayal on women. But it is the nature of discrimination to deform the favoured as well as the disfavoured. Many of us should rejoice for having been held by – or having married – or just knowing! – good fathers. Others of us need to recover absent fathers, or to forgive ourselves (or others) for being such. The presentation of Christ in the temple is a good occasion to do so.

Father in heaven
Your care for Joseph enabled him
To carry the salvation of the world on his shoulders.
Spread the glory of loving fatherhood widely on Earth.
Be tender where it has been missing
And plant it deeply in my soul.
In Jesus' name I ask.

THE TRANSFIGURATION OF CHRIST
ON THE MOUNTAIN

(seven weeks before Easter)

Mark 9: 2-8

Six days later, Jesus took with him Peter and James and John, and led them up a high mountain apart, by themselves. And he was transfigured before them, and his clothes became dazzling white, such as no one on earth could bleach them. And there appeared to them Elijah with Moses, who were talking with Jesus. Then Peter said to Jesus, 'Rabbi, it is good for us to be here: let us make three dwellings, one for you, one for Moses and one for Elijah.' He did not know what to say, for they were terrified. Then a cloud overshadowed them, and from the cloud there came a voice. 'This is my Son, the Beloved; listen to him!' Suddenly when they looked around, they saw no one with them any more, but only Jesus.

This reading emphasises to Christians that Jesus' ministry grows out of, and is continuous with, Judaism. The prayers below were prayed at St Martin-in-the-Fields on this day, which was 14 February, in 1999. The service was part of an annual series of inter-faith visits organised by the Council of Christians and Jews. In the week of the service, the first war crimes trial in the UK began.

Heavenly Father, you called Moses and Jesus into the cloud-covered mountains and disclosed your glory and power.
Generations before, you provided Abraham with a ram to sacrifice on the top of a mountain, so that it was said, 'On the mount of the Lord it shall be provided.'
We pray for all those who are called to high positions of religious and secular leadership. Awaken in each of us a sense of the mountains which you would have us climb; give us the persistence

and courage to meet you in lonely and inhospitable places; and
bless us, and our leaders, with the knowledge that on the mountain
of the Lord you will provide. *Lord, in your mercy: hear our prayer.*

In the first reference to mountains in the Bible, they are under
water. Noah was in his ark, and 'the waters swelled so mightily on
the earth that all the high mountains under the whole heaven were
covered'. Then the water subsides, and the ark rests on a mountain
top in Ararat. The whole landscape of life has been wiped away.
Noah only knows that there must be dry land somewhere when
the dove he releases comes back with an olive leaf in her beak.
Help all of us in those times when we are on the mountain top,
not transfigured in glory but fleeing in terror; when certainties and
security have been swept away; when normality is impossible. We
think of victims of natural disaster and victims of war; the victims
every day on our roads, and of abuse in families; and also those
who suffer from serious mental or physical illness. We pray for any
who strain daily for a dove bearing an olive leaf, but find none.
Lord, in your mercy: hear our prayer.

When Jesus was being tempted in the wilderness, the devil took
him up to a high place and showed him all the kingdoms of the
world and their splendour. 'All these I will give you,' the devil said,
'if you will fall down and worship me.' We see the devil and his
kingdoms nightly on the news. Heavenly Father, show us rather
the vision of Micah:
'In days to come the mountain of the Lord's house shall be
established as the highest of the mountains, and shall be raised up
above the hills. Peoples shall stream to it, and many nations shall
come and say: Come, let us go up to the mountain of the Lord, to
the house of the God of Jacob ... He shall judge between many
peoples, and shall arbitrate between strong nations far away; they
shall beat their swords into ploughshares, and their spears into
pruning-hooks; nation shall not lift up sword against nation,

neither shall they learn war any more.' *Lord, in your mercy: hear our prayer.*

This week, as the first war crimes trial in this country takes place at the Old Bailey, we think particularly of all those killed in Domachevo, Belarus, where on one day in September 1942 2,900 Jews were killed.

Bring them, and us, to the last high mountain in the Bible: the one in Revelation from which we see the holy city new Jerusalem coming down out of heaven, shining with the glory of God. It has a great high wall with twelve gates; and on the gates are inscribed the names of the twelve tribes of Israel. There shall be no more night, nor will they need the light of lamp or sun, for the Lord God will be their light, and they will reign for ever. *Lord, in your mercy: hear our prayer.*

Biblical references in these prayers are respectively to Genesis 22: 14; Genesis 7: 19; Matthew 4: 9; Micah 4: 1-3; Revelation 21: 10-12.

ASH WEDNESDAY

(the beginning of Lent, six and a half weeks before Easter)

Lent, which begins on Ash Wednesday, is the period of forty days leading up to Palm Sunday. It prepares for Holy Week – Jesus' entry into Jerusalem, his crucifixion and resurrection. Its example is the period of forty days and forty nights during which Jesus fasted in the wilderness before beginning his ministry. Ash Wednesday takes its name from a tradition of marking worshippers' foreheads with ash on that day, to symbolise the sins which Lent asks us to face.

'What is sin?' says a close relative of Pilate, but waits for no answer.

Bring into God's presence the crosses which you were given as a child. Picture them in young wood:
the crosses of your parents' expectations, or lack of them;
the crosses of material comfort or hardship;
the crosses of your body and of your physical appearance, which you felt acutely;
and the crosses fashioned for you in your education.

Almighty God, here are the crosses of childhood which I have carried: receive them from me.

Picture in thick timber beams, in load-bearing wood, the crosses of your adult life:
the crosses which you were given to carry, or out of ambition chose to carry, in working or in being denied work;
those patterns in the living out of relationships which you need to break, but cannot or do not;
the stresses of your temper and personality;
the opportunities given to others which you think should have

come to you;
and the responsibilities of caring for children or adults.

Almighty God, here are the crosses of adult life which I have carried: receive them from me.

Picture in splintering wood the crosses of sickness, bereavement and death. Think of the frailty of our created bodies, and any illness or distress which affects you or those whom you love. Bring into God's presence the crosses of all those known to you who suffer, and those who have died.

Almighty God, here are the crosses of sickness and death which I have carried: receive them from me.

Picture in carved wood, polished and decorated by generations, any crosses which you have been given by the church itself:
denial of your gender, race or sexuality;
poor teaching, ignorant advice or selfish use of power;
worship which suffocated your identity and your spirit.

Almighty God, here are the crosses of my religion which I have carried: receive them from me.

Picture in wood of your choice the crosses of your own creation: the crosses of your own sins. Feel their weight and length; their age or newness; with nature's roughness or carved by pride. Are these crosses the work of months or of moments? Where have you been keeping them? Whom have they hurt? What might it feel like to be without them?

Almighty God, here are the crosses of my own making: receive them from me and forgive me.

Creator God, you made us all out of infinite goodness. Out of infinite forgiveness you call us all to become our true selves in you. Burn these crosses, every one, to ash. Let their ashes be to us the seal of your forgiveness, the assurance of your power and the certain promise of new life.

PALM SUNDAY

(the Sunday before Easter)

These prayers follow the journey to Jerusalem and to the Temple which every Jew made every year at the approach of the Passover. This is the journey which Jesus made for the last time when the crowds greeted him with palms.

It is March. The rains have stopped but the ground is green. We are travelling towards Jerusalem – from every country, more than 100,000 pilgrims, towards a city where 25,000 people live.

Who are we? We are Israelites and Gentiles. Poor and rich. Priests and traders. Men and women. Lepers and slaves. Most of us walk for days, although a few of us have donkeys. But as we reach the gates of the Holy City, the lepers leave us, for they are outcasts and are not allowed in.

Heavenly Father, you are God of the outcast. The face of those whom we dare not face is your face. The limbs of those we would crush are your limbs. Those parts of ourselves which we will not admit are parts of you. We pray for all outcasts.

Lord in your mercy, hear our prayer.

We reach the Temple rapidly, for the city is only a kilometre across. The Temple is the marvel of our world, built of alabaster, marble and cedar wood, eighty years in its final construction; the work of construction employed at one time more than half the city.

We reach the court of the Gentiles, and a terrace five metres across bounded by a shoulder-high stone lattice. The Gentiles leave us now, for stone tablets in Greek and Latin warn them of death if they cross the lattice. On this terrace the sick most often sought Jesus' help.

Healing God, we pray for those who are sick or need help.

Lord in your mercy, hear our prayer.

We enter the court of Women, where hang golden lamps and golden bowls. At the western end rise fifteen semi-circular steps towards the fabulously beautiful Nicanor Gate, with doors of Corinthian bronze. Here Mary came after the birth of Jesus; here Jesus was presented and God's revelation was proclaimed by Simeon and Anna. Here women can go no further; so here the adult Jesus, who treated women with a new status, spent much time.

Almighty God, for your incarnation, first revelation, crucifixion and resurrection you trusted women to be closest to you; grant in our day and throughout your church that every gate, however historic and splendid, shall swing open for all women.

Lord in your mercy, hear our prayer.

Now we enter the court of Israel, the altar of burnt offering and, one metre higher up, the court of the priests. Here only sufficiently able-bodied Jewish men, if ritually clean, may enter. Here is the place of worship and sacrifice, and all the senses are assailed: salt, baking, wood fires and incense; harps, flutes, cymbals and singing. Here at Passover stand 7,000 priests in white linen vestments. Here, the slaughtering of 18,000 Passover lambs requires three "sittings". Here is the furthest that Jesus could go into the temple of his faith.

Lord Jesus Christ, through your new covenant you set an end to sacrifice. By your death you opened the way to a new priesthood not spattered in blood. Take the stain of human bloodshed away from all our dealings. Grant that the institutions, forces and instincts of bloodshed which surround us no more mesmerise us than the Temple mesmerised you. Let us sacrifice each other no longer.

Lord in your mercy, hear our prayer.

Finally we approach the sanctuary, by its porch; a building entirely covered in gold, fifty metres square. A concave mirror of gold reflects the rays of the rising sun to dazzle the entrance. Only priests may be here.

Now even priests must fall away. We are the high priest on the day of Atonement, and we walk down the sanctuary's twenty metre corridor. We reach the double curtain before the Holy of Holies. Woven in six colours, when the veil has to be purified, it takes 300 priests to wash it. We enter, alone and in the dark and by faith, into your presence.

Almighty God, we give thanks for those who have died. Be with us all at the moment of death, when we enter your presence, alone and in the dark. Give us the gift of trust; tear down the curtain of our fear; and wrap us in the radiant cloth of your resurrection and ours.

Merciful Father, accept these prayers for the sake of your Son, our Saviour Jesus Christ.

THE DIVINE PUZZLE AND THE LAST SUPPER

(Maundy Thursday, three days before Easter)

All four gospels make the betrayal of Jesus by one of the twelve disciples an integral part of his arrest and crucifixion. They link this betrayal to the last supper, remembered by Christians on the Thursday before Easter (and in every service of holy communion). Jesus says goodbye to his disciples, breaking bread, sharing wine and asking them to 'Do this in remembrance of me' (Luke 22: 19-20). What is *betrayal* doing here, so close to the heart of Christianity?

The betrayal of Jesus by Judas is a puzzle – a puzzle around the questions what, why and what if.

What did Judas betray? What was worth thirty pieces of silver to the priests of the temple? Was it identifying to the authorities who Jesus was, as Luke suggests when Judas picks out Jesus for the arresting party with a kiss (Luke 22: 48)? But only a few days before the crowds had recognised and greeted Jesus like a football star. In John's gospel Jesus steps forward himself as the arresters approach and says, 'I am he' (John 18: 6).

Did Judas reveal to the priests where Jesus would be? But Jesus would have been easy to find and to arrest. The garden of Gethsemane was a place where he 'often met … with his disciples' (John 18: 2). Jesus himself says, 'Have you come out with swords and clubs to arrest me as though I were a bandit? Day after day I sat in the temple teaching, and you did not arrest me' (Matthew 26: 55).

What would have been worth money would have been trial testimony from Judas as to what Jesus had said. The trial nearly collapsed for lack of evidence (Mark 14: 56). If Judas had been prepared to testify and agree with another witness as to what Jesus was teaching, that could easily have been worth money – say sixty pieces of silver, half in advance. But it does not happen. Jesus is convicted on words out of his own mouth during the trial.

It's the start of a puzzle – but only the start. Whatever Judas did betray, *why* did he do it? As commonly taught, Judas' motive was money (Matthew 26: 14). Doubtless some among the disciples had been money-motivated earlier in their lives, as some among any group of people might be. But after two years of travelling, baptising, preaching and healing with this essentially penniless prophet, not relying on money taken with them but sleeping overnight wherever they were given space on the floor, how likely is it that any of them would have been motivated by money now? Indeed, Judas returns the money before hanging himself (Matthew 27: 5).

Then, whatever Judas betrayed and for whatever reason he betrayed it, *what if* he had changed his mind? What if Judas had had an attack of conscience over supper? Suppose he had decided – just a few hours earlier than in fact he did – to give the thirty pieces of silver back to the priests. Visualise the scene. Jesus says goodbye to his disciples over bread and wine and leads them out across the Kidron valley to Gethsemane. He prays intently while they keep falling asleep, but the authorities do not come. What does he say in the morning? 'Anyone know where we can get some breakfast? And by the way, we've got a bit of a theological problem about the salvation of the human race.'

The betrayal by Judas handed down to us is like an arrangement of chess pieces two thousand years old which does not make sense.

It's hard to see how the pieces got to the positions in which we find them, if they followed the rules of chess (meaning here, the rules of human behaviour). It's tempting to decide that the puzzle has no meaning: that pieces have been stolen or added by passers-by, or that the board has been disturbed by centuries of over-zealous cleaners. There is no answer now: it's just life. How unlikely that any of us today would encounter a divine puzzle!

But if we did happen to take the puzzle seriously, we might pause on the use of the word *betrayal*. So Jesus characterises the act – 'Truly I tell you, one of you will betray me' (Mark 14: 18). Used widely the word can mean any serious breach of duty and trust. Jesus could have said of Peter, 'He betrayed me, he lied and he was not there for me when I needed him.' But denial or desertion are the words used instead, for what Peter says does not reveal something which is true, but asserts something which is false ('I do not know this man').

True betrayals imply not only that trust is broken but that in the wreckage something true is exposed – for example a hiding place, a confidence or an emotion ('his nervousness betrayed him'). *Only people who have secrets* can be betrayed in this narrower sense. The secret might be a "good" secret, one which a moral person would not want to expose, such as the Frank family's Amsterdam hiding place from the Nazis, but still there has to be a secret. So if Jesus was betrayed in this narrower sense, what was his secret, and what does it have to do with the last supper?

Here is a telling of the Judas story. It's a fantasy. No one can say whether it is true or not. But we can say whether it is a solution to the puzzle.

All the disciples whom Jesus had chosen were disciples in good faith. They followed him, they tried to understand him and sometimes they challenged his teaching.

During their journeys with Jesus they had seen visions and miracles. On a number of these occasions Jesus had told the disciples not to tell anyone about these "signs". On other occasions he had taught openly – especially about ethics – to hundreds of listeners. Over time the disciples, and then some of the people, started to think that Jesus might be the person promised in the Old Testament who would save the Jewish people. But it was far from clear what that would mean, even if it was true. Whenever the religious authorities tried to pin down Jesus about his authority or his role, he was renowned for his ability to subvert the question.

Inevitably one of the disciples was cleverer than the others; cleverer, and perhaps more disciplined. And if other disciples were prone to failings such as vanity and impetuosity, the weakness of this one was pride.

In the final days, Jesus prayed increasingly intensely, almost feverishly, well into the night. In doing so sometimes Jesus spoke aloud. Most of the disciples enjoyed their drink and were asleep. But to this particular disciple it was obvious that something was happening. The disciple tried to keep awake and sometimes he succeeded, keeping still for long night-time hours so as not to distract Jesus. After all, keeping awake was faithful discipline of the kind which Jesus had repeatedly urged – 'Keep awake therefore, for you know neither the day nor the hour' (Matthew 25: 13). It was hard, but the disciple felt sure that his efforts would bring a spiritual reward.

And so this disciple heard, or perhaps put together in his mind, that Jesus was grappling in prayer with a new stage of understanding of his relationship with God; that he was one with God in a unique way; one might even say that he was God. But was this madness speaking?

What a question to consider! But right and appropriate (thought this disciple) that God should have chosen the burden of thinking about it to rest on *his* shoulders, rather than those of colleagues who were vain, ill-disciplined or (no need to name names) a bit thick. So the disciple did not discuss this question with them.

This disciple did not lack vision or faith. If, unthinkable though it seemed, this man with whom they had been travelling was God, then something of this importance needed to be revealed without delay – for the good of all the people. On some nights the thought occurred to him, might not the disciple whose faith and ability had proved equal to discerning these great matters be given even greater responsibilities after the revelation – perhaps as head of a new church? And, which was a consoling thought to a clever person whose faith covered 92 per cent but not 100 per cent of the matter in question, if Jesus was not God but afflicted by growing delusions, without question it was any righteous person's duty to bring this nonsense to a rapid halt. A trial, where the question could be put to Jesus directly on oath, would resolve the matter elegantly.

The discussion with the priests was straightforward. Knowing that Jesus would assert his divinity if challenged on oath was easily worth thirty pieces of silver. It assured them that the trial would result in a conviction for blasphemy even if the witness evidence failed.

The last supper was both a goodbye and a hello. Jesus was with the disciples not only as someone familiar, but also as someone becoming new: someone more conscious than ever before of the divine plane and the human plane intersecting around him. At the divine level he knew that he would see his disciples again and be with them forever, but at the human level he wanted to leave something by which they could remember him. This "something" was also a hello as much as a goodbye – a way to touch and be touched by those believers who would come after. So Jesus broke bread, poured wine and with a few words shared them.

If the disciple's cleverness had managed to turn into wisdom, Jesus would have led his disciples out to pray and then taken them to the house of the high priest, to say what it had now come upon him to say. But the almost luminous quality of the meal only increased the disciple's excitement that something glorious would happen that night, and the cleverness of his plan would be at the heart of it. Jesus even said to him, 'Do *quickly* what you are going to do' (John 13: 27). Provided now he was quick, history would record that he was the disciple who had had vision, the one who had kept awake, the one who had been brave: the one who had unveiled the greatest revelation of God in human existence.

The clever disciple anticipated the revelation of God in his power and glory, or perhaps Jesus being revealed as human and deluded. He waited until the priests had posed the critical question. The resulting situation shattered his world: God revealed, but without power and glory. Judas did not wait for the crucifixion.

———————

Lord Jesus Christ
You hear our hearts before they beat.
In your hands are our thoughts before we wake
and our desires after dark.
Still you choose to stand beside us
Never tiring from finding what is good
or from accepting the pain.
With nothing left for us to say, just 'yes'
Help us to say it.

GOOD FRIDAY

(two days before Easter)

Good Friday commemorates the crucifixion of Jesus. He spends the last three hours of his life – from noon until 3 pm – on an execution cross, conscious, and occasionally speaking. If he spoke a little, he certainly thought and prayed much more. Present in his mind, and evidenced by his cry 'My God, my God, why have you forsaken me?' (a quotation from the psalms), would have been the holy writings of his faith – the Old Testament. The first five books of the Old Testament, collected together as the Torah or Jewish Law, date from the fourth century BC. The Prophets and other Writings in the Old Testament were added during the third to first centuries BC.

We cannot know what was in his mind, beyond pain. Quite possibly, if the pain allowed, for part of the time he would have thought about the account of creation with which the Old Testament opens; for Christians believe that on the cross God who was before all things and made all things was making a new creation.

The reflection which follows imagines thoughts in the mind of Jesus, the man on the cross, the man reliving his last days and the man addressing his Father in heaven; thoughts clear or near-delirious patterned by words which he had known from childhood (Genesis Chapter 1, the opening words of the Bible).

In the beginning when God created the heavens and the earth, the earth was a formless void and darkness covered the face of the deep, while a wind from God swept over the face of the waters. Then God said, 'Let there be light'; and there was light. And God saw that the light was good; and God separated the light from the darkness. God called the light Day, and the darkness he called Night. And there was evening and there was morning, the first day.

I have come as light, but the world loves the darkness.

I told my friends – You too are the light of the world! Let your light shine, so that others may see and give glory to God.

Perhaps I got a little carried away there. Can they be light, when they understand so little? They are so much more comfortable when I talk about sheep: can sheep turn into light?

And God said, 'Let there be a dome in the midst of the waters, and let it separate the waters from the waters.' So God made the dome and separated the waters that were under the dome from the waters that were above the dome. And it was so. God called the dome Sky. And there was evening and there was morning, the second day.

At the horizon the waters below and the waters above meet. The space between the two waters is the possibility for life. For your first promise, made to Noah, was that never again would you destroy all life. In that great flood, the waters below the sky and the waters above the sky were reunited, and all life was almost destroyed.

Will life survive? But you have willed not only survival but glory. You have willed that the human story will not be erased but perfected, with your eternal kingdom brought to all peoples and nations. Indeed, your will be done – though around me the people surge like a rising sea, and the authorities descend like a falling sky, and the space for my life between them is being rubbed out.

And God said, 'Let the waters under the sky be gathered into one place,
and let the dry land appear.' And it was so. God called the dry land Earth,
and the waters that were gathered together he called Seas. And God saw
that it was good. Then God said, 'Let the earth put forth vegetation: plants
yielding seed, and fruit trees of every kind on earth that bear fruit with the
seed in it.' And it was so. The earth brought forth vegetation: plants
yielding seed of every kind, and trees of every kind bearing fruit with the
seed in it. And God saw that it was good. And there was evening and there
was morning, the third day.

To be human is to forget as well as to remember. To remember
everything is to remember nothing.

Will they remember, 'I am the bread of life'? Will they remember
to be yeast, or only picnic baskets? Shall I ask them to break bread
to remember?

Will they remember, 'I am the true vine', or only the six stone
water-jars? Shall I ask them to share wine to remember?

They will remember and they will forget. Noah, the first wine-
grower, became drunk and lay naked, because he forgot; and Isaac
drank, and gave his blessing to Jacob and not to Esau because he
forgot; and your glory and your mercy Father abound in our
forgetting as well as our remembering.

And God said, 'Let there be lights in the dome of the sky to separate the
day from the night; and let them be for signs and for seasons and for days
and for years, and let there be lights in the dome of the sky to give light
upon the earth.' And it was so. God made the two great lights – the greater
light to rule the day and the lesser light to rule the night – and the stars.
God set them in the dome of the sky to give light upon the earth, to rule

over the day and over the night, and to separate the light from the darkness.
And God saw that it was good. And there was evening and there was
morning, the fourth day.

I wonder what it would have been like to have had children.
You promised children to our patriarchs, above all to Abraham –
'Look towards heaven and count the stars, if you are able to count
them. So shall your descendants be.'

I have been harsh on my family. I see my mother and she
remembers. 'Whoever does the will of God is my brother and sister
and mother,' is the saying of a young man too full of himself. Even
though it is true.

I wonder what it would have been like to have had children – even
though all the children that have been or will be, I have had.

And God said, 'Let the waters bring forth swarms of living creatures, and
let birds fly above the earth across the dome of the sky.' So God created the
great sea monsters and every living creature that moves, of every kind, with
which the waters swarm, and every winged bird of every kind. And God
saw that it was good. God blessed them, saying, 'Be fruitful and multiply
and fill the waters in the seas, and let birds multiply on the earth.' And
there was evening and there was morning, the fifth day.

Thank you for the sharing of life with friends. Especially Peter,
Andrew, James and John – the ones who were with me from the
beginning, fishing in the Sea of Galilee. 'Follow me, and I will
make you fish for people.' We have not lacked for crowds; nor do
we now.

Of all the things they still cannot see, that we are all your children, made in your image! 'Are not five sparrows sold for two pennies, yet not one of them is forgotten in your sight? Do not be afraid, you are of more value than many sparrows.' I seem to remember also trying ravens and lilies.

The time for speaking is ending now. Yesterday I washed their feet. They will surely remember the oaks of Mamre, where you appeared to Abraham as three angels. Abraham said, 'My lord, if I find favour with you, do not pass by your servant. Let a little water be brought, and wash your feet, and rest yourselves under the tree.' Abraham ordered water to be brought, but he himself did not wash your feet. I have washed *their* feet, and hope that even Peter can understand.

And God said, 'Let the earth bring forth living creatures of every kind: cattle and creeping things and wild animals of the earth of every kind.' And it was so. God made the wild animals of the earth of every kind, and the cattle of every kind, and everything that creeps upon the ground of every kind. And God saw that it was good.

Then God said, 'Let us make humankind in our image, according to our likeness; and let them have dominion over the fish of the sea, and over the birds of the air, and over the cattle, and over all the wild animals of the earth, and over every creeping thing that creeps upon the earth.' So God created humankind in his image, in the image of God he created them; male and female he created them. God blessed them, and God said to them, 'Be fruitful and multiply, and fill the earth and subdue it; and have dominion over the fish of the sea and over the birds of the air and over every living thing that moves upon the earth.' ... And it was so. God saw everything that he had made, and indeed, it was very good. And there was evening and there was morning, the sixth day.

Jonah you saved by a great sea creature, and Daniel you saved from the lions. Daniel's words haunt me, 'My God sent his angel and shut the lions' mouths so that they would not hurt me because I was found blameless before him.' Am I not blameless before you? When they brought me the woman guilty of adultery, no one came forward to condemn her; but now my life is fading, and the accusations raised against me make a sea.

I think of the angels and the wild beasts who waited on me in the wilderness, when we began this work. All the things you said then have come to pass. I remember the psalm I recited then:

'My God, my God, why have you forsaken me? …

Many bulls encircle me, strong bulls of Bashan surround me; they open wide their mouths at me, like a ravening and roaring lion.

For dogs are all around me; a company of evildoers encircles me. My hands and feet are shrivelled; I can count all my bones. They stare and gloat over me; they divide my clothes among themselves, And for my clothing they cast lots.

But you, O Lord, do not be far away! O my help, come quickly to my aid! Deliver my soul from the sword, my life from the power of the dog! Save me from the mouth of the lion!'

I'm glad I didn't understand it all fully then.

HOLY SATURDAY

(the day before Easter)

The reflection for Good Friday imagined thoughts of Jesus on the cross, patterned by the account with which the Bible opens of the creation of the world in six days, followed by the sabbath – the day of rest. This reflection for the sabbath before Easter takes a further step of imagination, beginning with the Genesis account of the first sabbath.

————————

Thus the heavens and the earth were finished, and all their multitude. And on the seventh day God finished the work that he had done, and he rested on the seventh day from all the work that he had done. So God blessed the seventh day and hallowed it, because on it God rested from all the work that he had done in creation.

'Come,' said the angel, so I got up and followed her.

'Where are we?' I said.

'The sabbath of desolation,' she replied. 'The space between the crucifixion and the resurrection.' The angel seemed to think this was an answer. I understood too little to disagree.

We climbed a ridge whose top we could not see. The sand, like the air, coated us in grime. For miles in every direction, the only signs of life – if indeed we were alive – were our own footprints.

After a while I said, 'This is a terrible place. Are we the only ones in it?'

Her eyes slapped me across the face. 'Oh no! In the future, whole centuries of mankind will choose to live here.' We stepped past a strange sight – a crushed box of metal in the sand, inscribed in some language "Coca-Cola" – and looked down into the valley behind the ridge.

This I never thought to see: a desert of centuries, and generations as numerous as the stars choosing to live here.

Their apartment blocks and houses and roads and shopping malls stretched to the horizon. 'These are the generations for whom the crucifixion has always happened but never the resurrection,' the angel explained.

Here in the sabbath of desolation are a people who have said, God is dead (or at least resting). Their understanding of the laws in nature is so full that of his inaction they need no convincing.

Theirs is a sabbath of isolation, where the empty places are full of people and the people are full of empty places.

Many things cannot be, or cannot be done, in this twilight life. The list of these things and the scribes of this temple who add to it are different, yet familiar to me. Here is a people who eat endlessly, but nothing nourishes. They heal miraculously, but are always sick. Everything is possible except to do good, because good does not exist. Here they understand everything, but nothing has meaning.

I became angry and turned to the angel saying, 'But I am the lord of the sabbath. When I was on this earth, when we were hungry we plucked grain and ate, though the scribes said we should not. When we encountered illness, we healed. We saved lives and forgave sins.

'I tell you, something greater than the temple is here. Even in the sabbath of desolation, my Father is still working and I also am working. Do you doubt that we shall finish our work? As I told you: who, intending to build a tower, does not first sit down and estimate the cost, to see whether he has enough to complete it? Otherwise, when he has laid a foundation and is not able to finish, all who see it will begin to ridicule him, saying, 'This fellow began to build, and was not able to finish.'

And the angel said, 'I do remember you saying something like that.'

EASTER DAY

*(the first Sunday following the first full moon of spring,
that is on or after 21 March)*

The reflection for Good Friday recalled the original creation in the
words of the first book of the Bible, in six days of labour followed by
the sabbath, the day of rest. The reflection for Holy Saturday recalled
that sabbath. On Easter Day we exult at the first day of God's new
creation, a new creation described and promised in words from the
last book of the Bible.

————

Almighty God

We exult and thank you for this heaven and this earth, which you
made for us as the cradle of our existence. After six days of creation
you declared, 'It is finished'. Though repeatedly we turned away,
you taught people in each generation to live by your faithful
promises.

We exult and wonder that to redeem all peoples and all creation
you sent your Son Jesus Christ as one of us. He died at our hands.
From the cross he declared 'It is finished.' Since then we have made
for ourselves a sabbath of desolation.

But your goodness and love cannot be contained, and now we
highly exult that you have raised Jesus from the dead. Your risen
Son is the promise and pledge of a new heaven and a new earth,
offered to all; a creation in which you will be as close to each one
of us as the evening breeze, yet we shall not hide. Alleluia, Christ is
risen! He is risen indeed, alleluia!

Then I saw a new heaven and a new earth; for the first heaven and the first earth had passed away, and the sea was no more. And I saw the holy city, the new Jerusalem, coming down out of heaven from God, prepared as a bride adorned for her husband. And I heard a loud voice from the throne saying, 'See, the home of God is among mortals. He will dwell with them: they will be his peoples, and God himself will be with them; he will wipe every tear from their eyes. Death will be no more; mourning and crying and pain will be no more, for the first things have passed away.'

I saw no temple in the city, for its temple is the Lord God the Almighty and the Lamb. And the city has no need of sun or moon to shine on it, for the glory of God is its light, and its lamp is the Lamb. The nations will walk by its light, and the kings of the earth will bring their glory into it. Its gates will never be shut by day – and there will be no night there.

Then the angel showed me the river of the water of life, bright as crystal, flowing from the throne of God and of the Lamb through the middle of the street of the city. On either side of the river is the tree of life with its twelve kinds of fruit, producing its fruit each month; and the leaves of the tree are for the healing of the nations. Nothing accursed will be found there any more. But the throne of God and of the Lamb will be in it, and his servants will worship him; they will see his face, and his name will be on their foreheads.

Then the one who was seated on the throne said to me, 'It is done! I am the Alpha and the Omega, the beginning and the end. To the thirsty I will give water as a gift from the spring of the water of life.'

The Spirit and the bride say, 'Come.' And let everyone who hears say, 'Come.' And let everyone who is thirsty come.

References for Jesus' sayings and Biblical accounts referred to in the reflections for Good Friday, Holy Saturday and Easter Day:

The first creation: Genesis 1:1-2:3
The first day: John 12:46; Matthew 5:14-16; John 3:19; John 10:11; John 8:58
The second day: Genesis 9:11 and 7:11; Mark 14:62; Daniel 7:13-14; Matthew 6:10
The third day: Matthew 13:24ff; John 6:35; Mark 8:14-21; Mark 14:22; John 15:1; John 2:1-11; Mark 14:23-25; Genesis 9:20-21; Genesis 27:25
The fourth day: Genesis 15:5; Mark 3:35; John 19:26-27; Mark 10:13-16
The fifth day: Matthew 4:18-22; Luke 12:6-7 and 24-28; Genesis 18:1-4; John 13:4-10
The sixth day: Jonah 1:17-2:10; Daniel 6:16-22; John 8:10-11; Luke 6:37; Psalm 22:1 and 12-21; Luke 23:46; John 19:30
The seventh day: Matthew 12:1-14; Luke 6:1-11; John 5:1-18; Luke 14:28-30
The new creation: Revelation 21:1-4 and 22-25; 22:1-4; 21:6; 22:17

APRIL FOOLS' DAY

(1 April)

A visitor about to be introduced to an egomaniacal ruler heard him roar with laughter and so said to herself, 'At least he has a sense of humour.' Alas, someone who laughs at *himself* has a sense of humour. Someone who laughs at others just has a sense of importance. Unlike Judaism, Christianity and Islam do not point out well that God, having invented the sense of humour, has one.

In the meantime here is a short guide to practical Christianity, found on an airline seat pocket card.

Grace and peace be to you, dear disciple, from the management and staff of Christian Airways.

We especially welcome our frequent prayer customers and hope that you appreciated the convenience of boarding last (or occasionally first), in accordance with the principle that 'the first shall be last and the last first'. Kindly bear with us as we work through slight teething problems in the application of this principle on a long-term basis. We also apologise if, owing to your having a reservation, we gave your seat to someone without.

Wherever you may be seated, many of our experienced travellers recommend some prior consultation with your neighbour before loving him or her as yourself.

Our whole company's purpose is to speed you to your destination, or in the event of an accident, to heaven. Should an early arrival in heaven not fit with your travel plans, do make use of the emergency exits provided.

An episcopal lifejacket (purple) with a self-inflating ego is provided under your seat. To attract attention, wear the large cross. Please do not inflate your ego while still inside the aircraft.

We are glad to reassure our women passengers that the provision of a full range of lifejackets for them continues to be a subject for lively and wholesome debate.

In the event of a landing on water, walking is recommended.

During your flight we look forward to offering you wine together with a wide array of loaves and fishes. We apologise if, due to previous disciple selection, your choice of food is not available. Please gather up any food left over until it fills all the baskets provided.

Finally, on your arrival we are pleased to offer you full participation at no extra charge in our award-winning physical baggage service. This service ensures that you do not become too attached to your material possessions. However rest assured that your theological baggage will always be delivered safely.

THE SOUTH LONDON SAMARITAN

(the murder of Stephen Lawrence, 22 April 1993)

Luke 10: 25-37

Just then a lawyer stood up to test Jesus. 'Teacher,' he said, 'what must I do to inherit eternal life?' He said to him, 'What is written in the law? What do you read there?' He answered, 'You shall love the Lord your God with all your heart, and with all your soul, and with all your strength, and with all your mind; and your neighbour as yourself.' And he said to him, 'You have given the right answer; do this, and you will live.'

But wanting to justify himself, he asked Jesus, 'And who is my neighbour?' Jesus replied, 'A man was going down from Jerusalem to Jericho and fell into the hands of robbers, who stripped him, beat him and went away, leaving him half dead. Now by chance a priest was going down that road; and when he saw him, he passed by on the other side. So likewise a Levite, when he came to the place and saw him, passed by on the other side. But a Samaritan while travelling came near him; and when he saw him, he was moved with pity. He went to him and bandaged his wounds, having poured oil and wine on them. Then he put him on his own animal, brought him to an inn, and took care of him. The next day he took out two denarii, gave them to the innkeeper and said, 'Take care of him; and when I come back, I will repay you whatever more you spend.' Which of these three, do you think, was a neighbour to the man who fell into the hands of the robbers?'

He said, 'The one who showed him mercy.' Jesus said to him, 'Go and do likewise.'

The Naked Year

Robbery along the roads leading to and from Jerusalem, a major commercial centre, was a well-known hazard in the time of Jesus. In addition to tithing to the priests a share (perhaps one or two per cent) of the agricultural harvest, every year Jews with land and cattle were required to bring one-tenth of their profits to spend in Jerusalem.

As for the Samaritans, having analysed despised trades and Jewish slaves, and then illegitimate Israelites and Gentile slaves, Joachim Jeremias writes: 'Descending to the lowest degree of the scale, we come to the Samaritans' (Jerusalem in the Time of Jesus, p 352). At the time Jesus was speaking, hatred had been freshly renewed: 'one Passover at the time of the Procurator Coponius (AD 6-9), some Samaritans strewed human bones in the Temple porches and all over the sanctuary in the middle of the night' (p 353).

At first glance the only connection between the murder of black teenager Stephen Lawrence at a bus-stop beside the Well Hall roundabout in south London on 22 April 1993 and the parable of the Good Samaritan is that the perpetrators escape justice. Stephen Lawrence is stabbed and bleeds to death in less than fourteen minutes in the road. The attacks take place not in a desolate place but in front of witnesses in a road 'thick with parked BMWs and Mercs. The road has two police stations: one down by Eltham High Street and one up by Shooter's Hill. Close to the second police station was Brook Hospital.' (Duwayne Brooks in 'Steve and Me', p 27). And of course the attacks on Duwayne Brooks and Stephen Lawrence are about racism, not robbery.

On 29 June 1998 the public inquiry chaired by Sir William Macpherson took evidence from one of the suspects, Jamie Acourt. Michael Mansfield QC, counsel for the Lawrence family, asks Acourt about the police surveillance video which Acourt has previously seen of Acourt's brother and friends.

MANSFIELD	Neil Acourt says, whilst picking up a knife from a window ledge in the room and sticking it into the arms of a chair says: 'You rubber-lipped cunt. I reckon that every nigger should be chopped up, mate, and they should be left with nothing but fucking stumps.' Now, Jamie, have you forgotten that?
JAMIE ACOURT	Yes, I have, yeah.
MANSFIELD	Right. Shocked, are you? An honest reply, please.
ACOURT	I ain't shocked. It is nothing to do with me. I ain't shocked.
MANSFIELD	David Norris is saying: 'I'd go down Catford and places like that, I am telling you now, with two submachine guns and, I am telling you, I'd take one of them, skin the black cunt alive, torture him, set him alight.' Then a little further down: 'I would blow their two legs and arms off and say, 'Go on, you can swim home now,' and he laughs. Neil Acourt, your brother, says: 'Just let them squirm like a tit in a barrel.' Do you find all this shocking?
ACOURT	I have no comment on it.

It is in this context that we have, for any Christian, the parable of the Good Samaritan – with the challenge of racism which the parable does also contain.

From the evidence to the Lawrence inquiry on 26 March 1998. Edmund Lawson QC is counsel to the inquiry, and Ian Macdonald QC is counsel for Duwayne Brooks.

CHAIRMAN   Thank you very much for coming. Mr Taaffe, you have been involved in giving evidence so much that I understand that your personal life has been disrupted.

LAWSON   Your name is Conor Andrew Taaffe, is it not?

TAAFFE   That's right, yes.

LAWSON   You and your wife had gone to a prayer meeting at the local Catholic church?

TAAFFE   Correct.

LAWSON   Then there came to your notice a couple of young black boys who were jogging along?

TAAFFE   … Mmm. When I say jogging, I didn't so much mean that I thought they were out jogging for exercise, just to sort of describe the pace. They seemed to be running. I did sense immediately something wrong, something dangerous, something suspicious straight away. It just – you just knew, you know.

LAWSON   You saw Stephen, to use your words, 'crash onto the pavement', is that right? … And [Duwayne Brooks] appeared to be trying to flag down passing cars?

TAAFFE   He was, yes.

LAWSON   Once you had appreciated, and very quickly you did, as your wife had said, that this was something serious, you went straight over towards where Stephen had fallen, did you not?

TAAFFE   Yes, yes … He was definitely still alive at that
                  stage …

TAAFFE   … When I went home – this isn't material but
                  I will say it anyway – I went home and washed
                  the blood off my hands with some water in a
                  container, and there is a rose bush in our back
                  garden, a very, very old, huge rose bush – rose
                  tree is I suppose more appropriate – and I poured
                  the water with his blood in it into the bottom
                  of that rose tree. So in a way I suppose he is
                  kind of living on a bit …

MACDONALD   Mr Taaffe, I think we all appreciate that you did
                  a wonderful thing that night. I just wanted to
                  ask you about the moment before you crossed
                  the road, you had some fears about what was
                  happening? You sensed danger … You thought
                  they might be about to commit a mugging or
                  something like that?

TAAFFE   The thought flashed through my mind, being
                  wary of the situation, that perhaps it was a ploy.
                  One would fall down and you would think: 'Oh
                  my God, there's something wrong.' You would
                  go over and the other might get you. That did
                  pass through my mind.

MACDONALD   Was that because it was two young black men
                  running along the other side of the road?

TAAFFE   I would say that that was part of my assessment,
                  yes.

(Reproduced from *The Colour of Justice* edited by
Richard Norton-Taylor, with permission of Oberon Books)

Heavenly Father
To have time or not to have time
To see or not to see
To know or not to know
To feel or not to feel
To cross over or not to cross over
To touch or not to touch
To be desolate or not to be desolate
To admit or not to admit
To be forgiven or not to be forgiven
To understand or not to understand
To forgive or not to forgive
To be or not to be.
The choice which you give us is the point of your creation:
Be with us when we choose.
In Jesus' name we ask.

HOLOCAUST MARTYRS REMEMBRANCE DAY

(27 Nisan)

The Holocaust remembrance day observed in Israel falls soon after Easter, on the twenty-seventh day of the Jewish month of Nisan. Following the Jewish lunar calendar, it marks the uprising in the Warsaw ghetto on Passover eve 1943 (19 April). A date falling soon after Passover was chosen for the commemoration. The poem 'Treblinka 1944' by T W Perkins is quoted from 'Beyond Lament' edited by Marguerite M Striar.

TREBLINKA 1944

Hope and faith are gone now.
Holidays pass, and no one worships.
Who is there foolish enough to pray
'To next year in Jerusalem'?
Who is there who still believes
they will live to see next year?

Only the strongest are still alive
even the strongest are weak now.
Too weak for hope,
too weak for prayer,
too weak for rituals;
surviving is itself a ritual:
the only one we know.

When the moon is red
the night I die
who will be left to see it?
My mother prayed over my sisters

my father over my mother.
I said Kaddish for my father.
Who will care to pray for me?

Now, as we march to our death
the ritual returns:
We say our final prayer
as we have done for ages.
Above the roaring fires
can be heard our chant:
'Hear, O Israel, the Lord our God,
the Lord is one.'

T W Perkins

Mourners and visitors enter the Children's Memorial at Yad Vashem by a concrete slope perhaps fifteen metres long. You enter a high, dark space, largely underground. The darkness hides your fellow guests; you may hold the railing tightly.

On every side, above and below, are invisible sheets of glass. Reflected in the glass, repeated to infinity in every direction, are five candle flames. The space is silent, except for a man's and a woman's voice, calling names. If we knew all the names there would be one and a half million of them, the children killed in the Holocaust.

Almighty God
Guide and inspire us so to live on this earth
that when the day comes for us to enter the place of darkness
we may find it to be none other than your infinite sea of light,
where all who have died are known by name
and the first of those names is your own.
In Jesus' name we ask.

ASCENSION DAY

(the fortieth day of Easter)

Ascension Day marks the end of the forty days during which Jesus appeared to those who had followed him. On this day (according to Acts 1:9) 'he was lifted up and a cloud took him out of [the disciples'] sight' or (according to Luke 24:51) 'While he was blessing them, he withdrew from them and was carried up into heaven.'

The date and authorship of the document reproduced below are not known.

PROPOSAL 9 TO THE COMMITTEE FOR THE PREVENTION OF GOD, FROM WORKING PARTY D (ON CHRISTIAN FESTIVALS)

SUMMARY: That we seek to divide the ending of Jesus' ministry from the empowerment of his followers, with the first event to be called if possible 'Ascension' and the second 'Pentecost'.

URGENCY: Urgent.

BACKGROUND:
Jesus did not teach theoretically. Time and again, his invitation and commandment was simple – 'Follow me'. Following his resurrection, he could have continued appearing to few or to many for decades and centuries, winning new adherents but creating a church of servants. But from the beginning he intended the empowerment of people as sons and daughters of God. He put the goal clearly, and noted that this goal would involve the ceasing of his own ministry on Earth: 'The one who believes in me will also do the works that I do and, in fact, will do greater works than

these, because I am going to the Father' (John 14: 12).

Jesus brought into the world a new spiritual authority. He seeks to transmit that authority and responsibility to the whole of humanity. In step one he arrives and says 'Follow me'; in step two he withdraws and says 'Go further'. And those who respond are provided with their own relationship with and empowerment from God to do this. 'Receive the Holy Spirit. If you forgive the sins of any, they are forgiven them; if you retain the sins of any, they are retained.' (John 20: 22-23)

Using our proposed terminology, the Ascension is the lightning flash of empowerment, of which Pentecost is the thunderclap – inseparable and dramatic. This is the divine intention. Therefore our task and opportunity is to separate them and make them obscure.

PROPOSED METHOD:

(1)   We shall encourage the Church to divide the empowerment act into two events as disconnected as possible: the cessation of Jesus' ministry and the gift of the Holy Spirit. Each on its own is easier to erode. We have received the interesting suggestion that if the first event were always to be celebrated on, say, a Thursday rather than a Sunday, its meaning might in time become lost altogether to the majority of the Church.

(2)   We propose to encourage that the first event be called 'Ascension'. This immediately takes the emphasis away from Earth, where the divine plan would have it, 'up' to heaven. The mind's eye cannot avoid the movement.

(3)   In a more scientific era, the emphasis on upward movement towards a heaven will help create the preconditions for

---

ludicrousness. To strengthen this, we hope the Church will be persuaded to adopt as a Bible reading to be read on 'Ascension' Day a passage about God being an old man with white hair in the sky (for example Daniel 7: 9).

(4) We propose that the second event should be called 'Pentecost'. This has enormous potential for becoming obscure. We also anticipate the assistance of generations of priests in maximising the diversion of attention onto wind, flames, tongues and operatic effects in general, rather than the empowerment of people directly by God.

(5) If these concepts receive the Committee's approval, we propose that the resulting actions should be referred to under the self-explanatory title, 'Project Helicopter'.

CHRISTIAN AID WEEK

(the second week in May)

During Christian Aid Week over 300,000 volunteers collect donations in Britain to tackle world poverty. One of a number of Christian development charities based in the UK, Christian Aid is known for its credo 'We believe in life before death'.

Letters from Jesuit missionaries sent home to Yugoslavia in the 1920s led Agnes Gonxha Bojaxhieu to become a nun in India, indeed to become an Indian, and to work among the poor of that country. In May 1929, aged eighteen, she was received as a novice at the Loreto Convent in Calcutta, taking the name Sister Mary Teresa. In May 1937 she took her final vows, from then on being known by the name by which she became famous – Mother Teresa, now beatified.

For Mother Teresa herself, the most significant day in her own life was 10 September 1946. Travelling by train from Calcutta to Darjeeling, she read the passage in Matthew's gospel in which Jesus asserts that in relation to feeding the hungry, welcoming the stranger, clothing the naked, taking care of the sick and visiting prisoners, 'Just as you did it to one of the least of these who are members of my family, you did it to me' (Matthew 25: 40).

She was seized by a vision of working for the poorest of the poor and living as one with them. Granted permission in 1948 to do this, she embarked with five rupees on a work which, in 1984, treated four million lepers, distributed rations to 106,000 people and cooked food to 51,000 more, tended 13,000 people dying destitute and looked after 6,000 babies. The order of Missionaries of Charity which she founded continued after her death on 5

September 1997. By 2001 the Missionaries of Charity served 'the poor and the unwanted, irrespective of caste, creed, nationality or race' in 123 countries.

To approach this achievement is to approach a spiritual vortex of immense power, whose scale dwarfs our mind and sense. To Mother Teresa, the scale was not the point at all. Her biographer T T Mundakel quotes her as saying (p 184), 'God has not called me to be successful. He has called me to be faithful.'

For her, the heart of everything was always the individual – and particularly the smile – the smile of a faithful person carrying out God's will with joy, and the smile of the person to whom God's love reaches out. Since respect for every person as an embodiment of God was the foundation stone of her work, Mother Teresa was intensely respectful of whatever faith the person she sought to help had (Mundakel, p 65):

Mother Teresa was always very particular that the dying should receive the rituals of their faith before they die – for Hindus, a little holy water from the Ganges on their lips; for Muslims, readings from the Holy Koran; for Christians, sacramental anointing, and so on.

Once, Mother Teresa picked up a man lying in the gutter and brought him to Nirmal Hriday. His body was full of festering wounds and nasty sores. She bathed him carefully, cleaned his sores, applied medicines and bandaged them, feeding him all the time with a dose of love and mercy. He never complained and he was not at all afraid of death. She prayed for him, and prayed with him, according to his faith. Slowly, hope of reaching heaven dawned on his face. He gave her a beautiful smile and said, 'All my life, I have lived in the street like a dirty animal; but now I am going to my eternal home like an angel,' and within three hours, he died a peaceful and beautiful death.

There is an immaturity which can often be seen in our teenage years but which may still drive us later on, when we meet someone out of the ordinary. It is the desire to copy them, and the connected assumption that they want us to copy them. In meeting the work of Mother Teresa, we can put both of these reflexes behind us. Although by 2001 her order had more than 3,500 sisters and about 400 brothers, she knew that only a tiny number of people are given by God the gift of devoting their whole lives to such selfless communion with the very poor. Why else are the careful and extended pathways of entry into any holy order there, but to challenge, to test and if need be to reject rather than to convert?

The challenges which Mother Teresa does pose to us are two, one beguilingly straightforward and the other full of deep mystery. One is to offer whatever we have to offer with a smile. The other is to be open to revolutionary possibilities in our own lives. If it is not quite obvious from life which of these two challenges is the straightforward one, and which is the deep, Mother Teresa's own opinion was clear (Mundakel, p 1):

'I know that true holiness consists in doing God's will with a smile, and so I have always tried to smile, even when things do not turn out as I would wish. Apart from that, I don't think I have done anything worth mentioning.'

———————

God of poverty and of smiles
Your eyes see many things.
The poverty of the cold and hungry, and the smiles of the smartly
casual.
The poverty of the sick and powerless, and the smiles of the valet
parked.
The poverty of the under-educated, and the smiles of the over-
photographed.

Help us also to see these poverties:
The poverty of being surrounded by riches, if you have to walk
fifty miles to find a generous person.
The poverty of being surrounded by information, if you can speak
to fifty people yet not find one who understands.
The poverty of being surrounded by smiles, if you can weep fifty
times without being heard by anyone who cares.

Put us to work in your world
With eyes that see reality
With hands and minds that change it
And with smiles which touch and transcend it.
In Jesus' name we ask.

PENTECOST

(seven weeks after Easter)

Pentecost, the Jewish festival on the fiftieth day after the second day of Passover, was a celebration of God's self-revelation through the giving of his Law to his people Israel. It is celebrated by Christians for the self-revelation and giving of God as Holy Spirit to his people (Acts 2). It is followed a week later by Trinity Sunday, which celebrates God the Father, God the Son and the God the Holy Spirit, one God.

An icon in words for Pentecost:

Eventually Pilgrim abandoned the torch. The night climb was fierce; a free hand was much more use in warding off gashes and bruises. It was June but he reached the top of Pentecost hill sufficiently before dawn to shiver in the chill.

As the first pink streaks appeared, he made out the cross on Easter hill due east. How far away was impossible to say: perhaps 2,000 years. Cosmic distances beyond, the sun was now rising rapidly. When Pilgrim's eye, the Easter cross and the nuclear fire of creation came into line, the cross was haloed in exploding light.

As to what happened next, Pilgrim had been warned but it was still quite confusing. A gust of wind blew past, slamming his eyes shut and sucking the air out of his lungs; the ground shook; and he saw tongues of fire. And after the wind, the earthquake and the fire, an incredible sensation which afterwards he could only describe as – as – well, a *caress*.

May we accept again today the Divine Gift from the Creator who gives us our own expression in existence, and from God Incarnate who gives us his own expression in Jesus. May the one indivisible God lift us to see visions and to dream dreams; to know more of the truth than previously we could bear; according to Jesus' promise, to do even greater works than he did; and more than these things, to know love.

TRINITY SUNDAY

(eight weeks after Easter)

God the Holy Trinity – Father, Son and Holy Spirit equal and one
– tells us that in the fulfilment of all things, human identity and
individuality is not lost but perfected, because Jesus' own identity as
part of the Trinity is not lost but perfect. In the opening verses of
John 14, Jesus tells us:

'In my Father's house there are many dwelling-places. If it were
not so, would I have told you that I go to prepare a place for you?
And if I go and prepare a place for you, I will come again and will
take you to myself, so that where I am, there you may be also.'

Trinity Sunday tells us that when we go to heaven it is not as
snowflakes falling onto a bed of snow, whiteness lost in a sea of
greater whiteness, but as blazing shafts of different colours, jewels
individually cut, set in a palace of unimaginable colour.

Here is our Father's house of many dwelling-places, the new
Jerusalem, described in Revelation 21:

'The foundations of the wall of the city are adorned with every
jewel; the first was jasper, the second sapphire, the third agate, the
fourth emerald, the fifth onyx, the sixth cornelian, the seventh
chrysolite, the eighth beryl, the ninth topaz, the tenth chrysoprase,
the eleventh jacinth, the twelfth amethyst ... And the city had no
need of sun or moon to shine on it, for the glory of God is its light
and its lamp is the Lamb.'

Desmond Tutu, Archbishop emeritus of Cape Town, has called us
to be the rainbow people of God. Trinity Sunday calls us to realise
that we are the people of a rainbow God.

THE DEATH OF EMMELINE PANKHURST

(14 June)

Emmeline Pankhurst, leader in the campaign for women's equality with men, died at a nursing home in Wimpole Street on 14 June 1928.

Humans only build in cemeteries. What we can see today; what we can think today; who we can be today; we know all of it is built of, and upon, the bones of others who went before us.

When Emmeline Pankhurst died aged sixty-nine, something of profound importance to her life's work and to subsequent British life was achieved. On the day of her funeral, royal assent was given to the bill which gave women in Britain the vote at age twenty-one on fully equal terms with men. Ten years earlier in 1918, women aged at least thirty and subject to other restrictions had first gained a national vote.

Campaigning and organising, suffering repeated imprisonment and illness, she was not alone. British women gained the right to vote because, among other things, over a thousand women suffragettes went on hunger strike in prison. In twentieth-century Britain, they endured being force-fed by Government order through the nostril, the mouth, the rectum and the vagina.

From 1886 a majority of MPs had been reported to be in favour of votes for women, but no legislation was passed. Different leaders devised different strategies in response. Pankhurst created and put her stamp on a form of militancy, defining its boundaries and directing its use. The groups she led broke windows, poured acid on mail in pillar-boxes, assaulted police officers, went on hunger strikes and committed arson on property.

As it had to be, it was also a struggle of words and concepts. There were arguments on both sides. In 1892 Asquith, who would be Prime Minister at the height of suffragette militancy, set out the four reasons why women should not have the vote: that the vast majority of women did not want it; that they were not fit for it; that women operated by personal influence; and that it would upset the natural order of things.

In the battle of words Pankhurst became a noted orator. She rallied women and men across all classes, and later on both sides of the Atlantic. In vision, in sacrifice, in rhetoric, in devising and pursuing a contentious strategy for change in the midst of partial democracy, in enfranchising millions, Emmeline Pankhurst's accomplishments rank with those of – say – Martin Luther King. But there is a version of history in which only one of them has a dream. We regard and remember differently the dreams, words and achievements of men and of women.

Is any of this a *religious* problem? Only if there exists a God who cares as much for the dreams, words and achievements of daughters as for those of sons. Of course if such a God exists, then according to the Christian revelation there is a specifically religious word for so deeply embedded a distortion in humanity. It is sin.

Whether this creation is one in which St Paul and Emmeline Pankhurst will one day meet I do not know (though if they do, perhaps in some heavenly chat show, tickets for the encounter sold out some time ago). But St Paul describes in haunting language what it is to have one's eyes opened to sin which is not simply individual but structural. And as both postscript and call to action: does either of their lives (Pankhurst's or St Paul's) leave room for much doubt as to the difference to things structural which one person's life can make?

Romans 8: 19-23

For the creation waits with eager longing for the revealing of the children of God; for the creation was subjected to futility, not of its own will but by the will of the one who subjected it, in hope that the creation itself will be set free from its bondage to decay and will obtain the freedom of the glory of the children of God. We know that the whole creation has been groaning in labour pains until now; and not only the creation, but we ourselves, who have the first fruits of the Spirit, groan inwardly while we wait for adoption, the redemption of our bodies.

Almighty God
We acknowledge before you our historic, deep-rooted and continuing failure – as men and as women – to acknowledge the image of you in women on equal terms with that in men.
Forgive us and transform us – women and men – into angels of your love and light:
Unafraid of systems, principalities or powers
Unafraid of men
Unafraid of women
And unafraid of ourselves.
In Jesus' name we ask.

MIDSUMMER, PAGANS AND PLATO

(21 June)

The summer solstice, the longest day in the northern hemisphere and in terms of light the turning point of summer, occurs on 21 June – a significant moment for almost any form of life on Earth, and therefore in any pagan calendar.

Chronologically Christianity is the "middle child" of the family of three religions which descended from Abraham, sandwiched between the older Judaism and the younger Islam. That photograph of three monotheisms sitting on a park bench is indeed very useful in nurturing much needed respectful dialogue between the three of them. However it is at least as important in modern Britain to dust off a different photograph: the one which has paganism and Plato leaning their bicycles against the wall of a country pub, with the young upstart Christianity squeezing in at the side of the picture. Without a glimmer of understanding about that within us which can be called pagan, or that which out of respect and convenience is usually ascribed to Plato, we make it harder to understand what is Christian.

Paganism identifies religions which see divinity or spirituality in nature. This is a very ancient, possibly universal, religious understanding. Christians do well not to abuse it – if only not to abuse the parts of that understanding within ourselves. And it is not something long ago and far away.

During 1995, while assembling and publishing Britain's 100 most popular poems, the BBC broadcast an anonymous poem. It had been found in an envelope left for his parents, to be opened in the

---

event of his death, by a soldier killed in Northern Ireland. Its origin has not yet been traced, but the public response which it provoked was so strong that the BBC decided that the poem deserved listing ahead of the formal competition winner (Rudyard Kipling's 'If'). The poem reads:

DO NOT STAND AT MY GRAVE AND WEEP

Do not stand at my grave and weep;
I am not there. I do not sleep.
I am a thousand winds that blow.
I am the diamond glints on snow.
I am the sunlight on ripened grain.
I am the gentle autumn rain.
When you awaken in the morning's hush
I am the swift uplifting rush
Of quiet birds in circled flight.
I am the soft stars that shine at night.
Do not stand and my grave and cry;
I am not there. I did not die.

(Anonymous: reproduced from *The Nation's Favourite Poems* with permission from BBC Worldwide Ltd)

This is a beautiful poem – a beautiful pagan poem. To state this is not to attack it, or to cut Christians off from it; it is to be honest about the springs of our spirituality in Britain near the start the twenty-first century. As Christians we can easily read the poem with love, seeing in our perspective the Creator God, the Risen Lord and the Holy Spirit shining through every line of it. The poem itself says something simpler and more accessible than this. But it is not something profoundly contradictory to Christianity, because Christianity asserts the preciousness of all creation, all being owing its existence to the one God, all waiting for life and meaning beyond the "now".

In its effects on our spirituality, the thought of the Greek philosopher Plato (circa 428 – 348 BC) is also not something long ago and far away. He particularly expressed a division between the immortal soul and the mortal body, giving us a knife which we still use to cut our very beings into two today. You can watch the surgery taking place in front of your eyes, to the sound of soaring music, in this song by Mike Scott of the Waterboys (recorded in 1985 on their album 'This is the Sea'):

SPIRIT

Man gets tired
Spirit don't
Man surrenders
Spirit won't
Man crawls
Spirit flies
Spirit lives when man dies

Man seems
Spirit is
Man dreams
The spirit lives
Man is tethered
Spirit is free
What spirit is man can be.

Powered by the music, these words create a picture of halls of meaning and eternity so much more important than our cramped, limited, mortal existences: places to which we can soar, and (we may feel) to which we are meant to soar. This also is not a Christian view of the world, although a Christian might feel that it does open up a view beyond snow, stars and grain which needs to be opened up.

In fact, although Christian thought and life down the centuries has borrowed both from pagans and Plato, with much more hostility expressed towards the former, the greater tension should be between Christianity and Platonism. Devaluing material existence relative to the "spiritual" devalues what, in Christianity, God has made and has affirmed in its sacredness by entering through his own incarnation.

Returning to the photograph with the bicycles, Christians can be less inhibited (and more respectful) about celebrating with pagans the divine in the snow, the stars and the grain. We can, with Platonists, have our eyes opened to halls of meaning and eternity beyond these things – but we need to keep an eye on that knife. Recognising more precisely what their faith is, Christians can offer for celebration heaven and earth together, created and redeemed by the one eternal God. In every one of us and in his incarnation God reverses Mike Scott's song: what man and woman is, spirit has dared to be.

GAY PRIDE

Gay Pride is the only annual celebration, civic or religious, of *any* kind of sexuality in our society. This reflection and prayer address sexuality in a broad sense.

700 people took part in the first Gay Pride march in this country on 1 July 1972. Similar events have taken place in London annually since (in 1999 briefly renamed Mardi Gras). Gay Pride events take place in many places in July or August. An estimated 60,000 people attended in Hyde Park in London on 26 July 2003.

It would be hard to pick two more explosive words for Christians than "gay" (meaning homosexual) and "pride", let alone putting the two together. But as Christians with whatever perspective on homosexuality, we can use this distinctive event to ask a broader question. Why do we not more passionately celebrate sexuality as a gift from God?

One response would be that we live in an alreadily heavily sexualised society. Since our society does sex so heavily there is no need for churches to do more. This point of view explains neither the absence of any civic celebration of sexuality more broadly than homosexuality, nor why other subjects of which society already makes a big fuss – for example motherhood, the Royal Family or the nation – often feature in church liturgy.

Another response might be that Christianity only celebrates sexuality within marriage, and churches do indeed make a big fuss about marriage. So far, so good. That so few Sunday pew sheets announce the formation of church groups of married people to study the Song of Solomon (the most sexual book in the Bible) is, on this view, accidental. It just happens that church fêtes need all that space and more to solicit the making of jam.

A third suggestion would be that whatever the minds and hearts of individual Christians, the public agenda of Christianity is dominated by institutions and, in some of those institutions, priesthoods. On this view these structures, still largely dominated by men who have defined their identities and vocations as religious, remain collectively scared rigid of sexuality for reasons which have as much to do with institutional tensions (not to mention newspaper investigations and law suits) as with theology. Now, Mrs Robinson, enough of sexuality: how about a nice harvest festival instead?

Each of us receives and unwraps our own sexuality as a gift from God of fundamental significance. After all Christianity is an incarnational religion, and giving thanks for sexuality is simply part of treating the physical creation and life lived within it as of sacred importance.

The Song of Solomon (1: 2 – 'Let him kiss me with the kisses of his mouth!') is an easy Biblical resource on sexuality, but Ecclesiastes may have more staying power. Solomon's lovers are relentlessly young ('be like a gazelle or a young stag' is the final verse) in a way which is almost cousin to the commercialised sexuality which surrounds us.

The sexuality which is of God enjoys youth, but it ages. It touches all, tastes all, breathes all and sees all. It comes to understand and to make luminous with love the creatureliness of all ages. Ecclesiastes expresses this quality. This allegorical description of old age, with eyes that shut, teeth that grind no more, hair that whitens and legs that stumble, describes an old age which has not forgotten death or youth, nor has it become embittered about either. The passage breathes freedom; but it is a real freedom, and therefore a freedom with consequences.

Ecclesiastes 11: 7 – 12: 7

Light is sweet, and it is pleasant for the eyes to see the sun. Even those who live for many years should rejoice in them all; yet let them remember that the days of darkness will be many. All that comes is vanity.

Rejoice, young man, while you are young, and let your heart cheer you in the days of your youth. Follow the inclination of your heart and the desire of your eyes, but know that for all these things God will bring you into judgement. Banish anxiety from your mind, and put away pain from your body; for youth and the dawn of life are vanity.

Remember your creator in the days of your youth, before the days of trouble come and the years draw near when you will say, 'I have no pleasure in them'; before the sun and the light and the moon and the stars are darkened and the clouds return with rain; on the day when the guards of the house tremble, and the strong men are bent, when the women who grind cease working because they are few, and those who look through the windows see dimly;

when the doors on the street are shut, when the sound of the grinding is low, and one rises up at the sound of a bird and all the daughters of song are brought low; when one is afraid of heights and terrors are in the road; the almond tree blossoms, the grasshopper drags itself along and desire fails; because all must go to their eternal home, and the mourners will go about the streets;

before the silver cord is snapped and the golden bowl is broken, and the pitcher is broken at the fountain, and the wheel broken at the cistern, and the dust returns to the earth as it was, and the breath returns to God who gave it.

Creator God and lover of humankind
Thank you for your gift to me of my sexuality.
When sexuality is troubling
Just as when it flows confidently and unchecked
Hold me and keep me.
Keep strong my concern for others
Make me an instrument of life to them
And from emptiness deliver me.
In Jesus' name I ask.

THE ATOMIC BOMB IS DROPPED ON NAGASAKI

(9 August 1945)

By 9 August, the effects of the first atomic bomb dropped at Hiroshima on 6 August 1945 killing 130,000 people were already apparent.

The visibility over the city was extremely poor. Moments after 11am local time the B29 Superfortress 'Bockscar' was down to its last two or three minutes of fuel before having to return to base. Suddenly the clouds opened up and Major Charles Sweeney saw the huge Nagasaki Mitsubishi arsenal plant. While the plutonium bomb fell through about eight kilometres of sky to detonate about half a kilometre above the Mitsubishi sports stadium, not far from the Catholic cathedral, there would have been about a minute of silence.

In one minute of silence, we make our own cry to God our Father.

WEDDINGS AND COMMITMENT CEREMONIES

Weddings are not the same as commitment ceremonies, for many reasons. One reason is that commitment ceremonies can be entirely individual and so quite different from each other, not only in symbol but in what is symbolised. I wrote this prayer for the commitment ceremony of my sister and her partner on 22 August 2002. It is reproduced here with their permission.

———

Almighty God
In the desert's silence, you are there.
In an orchid's whisper, you are there.
In the thunder of a volcano, you are there.
And when we dare face our dreams and fears, you are there, for you made us in your own image.

You made us, and make us, through the tensions, the possibilities and the limitations of relationships. We bring before you all those here, elsewhere and departed, who are part of us or have shaped us. We acknowledge the bruises and the hugs; the acceptance and the rejection; what was and what never had the chance to be.

Sorrowfully we think of the frustration of your creativity expressed in human life caused by fear and prejudice of all kinds. We celebrate and thank you for all those who have challenged those evils and so made different possibilities real.

And now we pray that you make real from today a different possibility of life together for Catherine and Jo. May they never lose sight of their own, and each other's, potential for growth – for you are a relentless, creative God. And in a thousand ways, but not least through each other and through us, may they know even more surely your unconditional presence and love.

In the desert's silence, you are there.
In an orchid's whisper, you are there.
In the thunder of a volcano, you are there.
And now as Jo and Catherine choose to face their dreams and fears together, you are here, for you make us in your own image.

EXAMINATIONS

Except for fighting wars, paying taxes and changing the clocks twice a year, receiving the results in August of national school-leaving examinations are perhaps the last thing which a rising generation in this country does altogether, all at the same time.

It is a rite of passage which deserves a thought and some celebration. For those who sit them, the examinations are a set of points on a railway track. In some cases they are passed without hesitation or interruption. In other cases something sudden, impersonal (and fallible) intervenes to cause a life shift.

But the larger scene of what happens in educational terms every August is almost magical. Even more than on electricity, transport or money, our civilisation is built on learning and on the transmission of knowledge. This is true even for the survival of religious faiths. In each new generation that exploding body of understanding has to be re-created from nothing. In the perspective of the universe, all human knowledge and self-understanding flickers a millisecond away from extinction.

So while in August we may be tempted to say that this year's TV game shows are even worse than last year's, or to speculate that the rise in A level scores achieved by young people may be a consequence of global warming, nonetheless something amazing is happening in front of our eyes.

Almighty God

Thank you for good teaching and good learning – the glory of
every human civilisation. Thank you for all those who work in our
education and examination systems to make them a blessing. We
pray for everyone receiving examination results and for everyone
who supports them and will advise them.

Above all, we thank you for nurturing within the vast emptiness of
space and time our fragile community of human knowledge and
meaning. We add with delight a new generation to that
community.

This new generation will come to know marvellous things which
we cannot imagine, so we celebrate with them.
In new knowledge they will find new opportunities for service, so
we thank them.
In new challenges they will confront new evils, so we pray for
them.

In Jesus' name we ask.

GETTING OUT OF IT

Getting "out of it" is so endemic in our culture, that this reflection could have been placed at more or less any point in the year. Here at the end of August it could connect with bank holiday raves, clubbing in the Mediterranean or, coming after the previous piece, getting smashed after examinations.

———————

Christianity's relationship with intoxication is not straightforward. Consider its sibling, Islam. Intoxication, and the production of and trade in intoxicants, is forbidden in Islam. The massive loss of lives and parts of lives which widespread "substance" use and abuse causes in us and around us makes stacking up the evidence for such a stance easy.

Even the making of containers (such as brandy glasses) for intoxicants is forbidden in Islam. How different in Christianity to use wine sacramentally. How different for Jesus to teach 'I am the vine and you are the branches.'

Jesus did not have in mind making grape jam. The Bible's view is that intoxication has been a feature of human culture at least since the Flood. Noah is the first planter of vineyards and within the next verse he is drunk (Genesis 9: 20-21). The early version of the Atkins diet adopted by John the Baptist, who neither ate bread nor drank wine, is not copied by Jesus (Luke 7: 33-34). Quite the reverse: Jesus chooses bread and wine together to be carriers of divinity in the Eucharist.

Of course even at its most innocuous drunkenness makes one drowsy, self-absorbed and inattentive, and the Gospels warn against that many times. But stand that against the first miracle of Jesus recorded in John's Gospel: the turning of 120-180 gallons of water into wine for the wedding-feast whose supplies had run out (John 2: 1-11). Size matters: the problem at Cana was not that guests would receive *nothing* to drink, and so be excluded from an important ceremonial. Rather, that the guests had already drunk dry the cellars of a host who could afford many servants – but wanted to drink some more.

Those of us who have heard this passage read so many times by people who appear to be the epitome of sober niceness may miss quite a large point. Try the wedding-feast again with a difference: had Jesus lived in a society where the use of ecstasy was accepted, would he have made more ecstasy when initial supplies had run out? (Anyone who is sure they know the answer, should consider why they are so sure.)

In perverse circumstances, intoxication could be healthier than its opposite. During the Vietnam war, American authorities became concerned at the proportion of their soldiers who used heroin, fearing for society on their return; but mostly, when the war ended so did the heroin use. Would it have been healthier, or morally better, for them to do what they did unintoxicated? The key to removing the heroin was to remove the napalm.

Of course the life-and-death question which this begs is whether those soldiers should have done, or been expected to do, what they did. And perhaps it is the same, equally life-and-death, question which is begged about our own society which medicates itself so heavily with such destructive effect. Perhaps we should fixate less on the supply of and demand for intoxicants as if these were subjects unconnected to any other, and ask more pointedly why the capacity of our rational, accountable, independent selves to find bliss with others has so atrophied as to require floating on such a vast chemical sea. Should we search less for the heroin in our society and more for the napalm? If "getting out of it" is the pandemic response, might building a society honeycombed through and through with isolation cells for the soul be the pandemic cause?

Almighty God
We pray for the millions of adults and children who suffer, directly or through those to whom they are close, from alcoholism, drug abuse or any other addiction.
Help them through this day.
For us and for them, be strength and inspiration for new life.
Lead us to question our own part in making of our own lives a place where so many of us prefer not to be.
In Jesus' name we ask.

THE DESTRUCTION OF THE WORLD TRADE CENTER

(11 September 2001)

History may rank the destruction of the World Trade Center in some league-table of evil or it may not. No matter: we are no jury shortlisting '9/11' for the "Booker Prize" of terrorism. We are the first generation on this planet to have watched, from every continent, as it happened, thousands of fellow human beings being killed. Some of us wept, some were numb, some wanted to kill and some applauded. Whether we remember, and what we remember, judges us.

One photograph in a book published to mark 11 September 2001 shows part of one side of the World Trade Center's north tower – a fragment of four floors – shortly before the tower collapsed. Smoke is streaking from the windows which people have smashed, and people are leaning or clambering out of the windows. With difficulty you may count twenty of them. They are the tip of a human iceberg which is about to disintegrate.

To remember inadequately is a kind of lie. We need to remember the people who were crushed in the buildings and on the aircraft; those who tried to rescue them; those who received telephone messages from hell and those who searched for days receiving no message at all; and the children left behind.

In the same book are twin photographs showing the same Manhattan skyline on 30 August and 27 September 2001. For me, the now-missing towers suggest twin questions which arise from the devastation: for what should I be prepared to kill? And for what should I be prepared to die?

Dear God
Pour out your love and your hope on this sometimes hellish world;
a world in which so many people in so many places – in America,
in Iraq, in Israel, in Palestine and elsewhere – are parched and
dying for lack of either of them.

———

The prayers which follow were used in a multi-faith service at St
Martin-in-the-Fields on 8 September 2002.

At this time of international concern we lift the hopes and fears of
the world to you, O God. The response to the prayers comes from
Africa. It is 'Your will be done on earth O Lord', in Xhosa.

God of Abraham
You taught your people through faith and through suffering.
Strengthen our faith in you and our understanding of you.
In the face of flames of anger
In the face of explosions of hate
In the face of terrorists who say, 'I shall smash your world'
Give us grace to say: God of faith, your will be done.
Mayenziwe 'ntando yakho

Lord Jesus Christ
You showed your people love and forgiveness beyond our
imagining.
When our lives are in ashes
When our city is in ruins
When we want to say to the terrorists, 'We shall smash your world'
Give us grace to say: God of love, your will be done.
Mayenziwe 'ntando yakho
God of Muhammad
You challenged your people to hope and to struggle for a better
world.

When this task seems impossible
When our imaginations are empty
When our words have died
Give us grace to say: God of hope, your will be done.
Mayenziwe 'ntando yakho

HARVEST FESTIVAL

(a Sunday at the end of September or beginning of October)

She said, 'You're cheating. You've left out all the bits about weeping and gnashing of teeth. About being thrown into the fiery flames. About hell.'

'The piece for the holocaust was quite hellish,' he replied. 'Some fiery flames there.'

'That's not the same thing at all,' she pointed out at once. 'The holocaust is us throwing each other into the flames. Hell is where *God* does the throwing.'

'All right then,' he conceded. 'The fiery flames – the weeping and gnashing of teeth – the whole thing. A harvest reflection.'

———————

Matthew 13: 24-30, 36-42, 47-50:
He put before them another parable: 'The kingdom of heaven may be compared to someone who sowed good seed in his field; but while everybody was asleep, an enemy came and sowed weeds among the wheat, and then went away. So when the plants came up and bore grain, then the weeds appeared as well. And the slaves of the householder came and said to him, 'Master, did you not sow good seed in your field? Where, then, did these weeds come from?' He answered, 'An enemy has done this.' The slaves said to him, 'Then do you want us to go and gather them?' But he replied, 'No; for in gathering the weeds you would uproot the wheat along with them. Let both of them grow together until the harvest; and at harvest time I will tell the reapers, Collect the weeds first and bind them in bundles to be burned, but gather the wheat into my barn.'

Then he left the crowds and went into the house. And his disciples approached him, saying, 'Explain to us the parable of the weeds of the field.' He answered, 'The one who sows the good seed is the Son of Man; the field is the world, and the good seed are the children of the kingdom; the weeds are the children of the evil one, and the enemy who sowed them is the devil; the harvest is the end of the age, and the reapers are angels. Just as the weeds are collected and burned up with fire, so will it be at the end of the age. The Son of Man will send his angels, and they will collect out of his kingdom all causes of sin and all evildoers, and they will throw them into the furnace of fire, where there will be weeping and gnashing of teeth.

'Again, the kingdom of heaven is like a net that was thrown into the sea and caught fish of every kind; when it was full, they drew it ashore, sat down and put the good into baskets but threw out the bad. So it will be at the end of the age. The angels will come out and separate the evil from the righteous and throw them into the furnace of fire, where there will be weeping and gnashing of teeth.'

There are some facts about Christianity which show it quite objectively to be different from most other religions, and really rather extraordinary. Unfortunately one of those facts is that every autumn somewhere near you in Britain there will be an act of divine worship which includes a tin of supermarket own brand peas.

In an act almost of cultural hooliganism, what would be a natural and colourful pagan celebration of harvest and of the powerful annual cycle of life – all reds and golds of autumn fruit and leaves – has been sacrificed by Christians to no very good end. First, it has been domesticated. Then, with just a subtle shift of attention towards man's rather than nature's activity in the harvest, what is left is a "religious" celebration of the principles that you-reap-what-you-sow, that God-likes-people-like-farmers-who-get-up-very-early-in-the-morning-and-work-hard and, for good measure, if-there-are-a-lot-of-nice-things-around-it's-best-to-store-them-away-because-hard-times-are-doubtless-coming.

These harvest principles are very potent. Most organisations depend utterly upon them; even countries try to run on them. Some people call them the Protestant work ethic. However that may be, Jesus spent much of his time pointing out that these principles have very little to do with the kingdom of heaven. Jesus called men and women to a heaven which is a far more reckless place where prodigal children are fêted, where a woman pours out precious ointment on Jesus and does not sell it for the poor, where labourers who only work in the afternoon are paid the same full day's wages as those who worked from the morning, where earth is not a wise place to store up treasure and where lilies of the field which neither toil nor spin are clothed in glory greater than Solomon.

Jesus does have things to say about harvest. The harvest which exercises him is the day of judgement – the harvest of souls at the end of time, to be sorted according to whether they have brought forward good or bad fruit. About this harvest he says two things – insistently, vividly, melodramatically, indeed in any way in which he can capture his hearers' attention. First, that the moral quality of what each of us does, thinks and says day by day is a matter of urgent and lasting importance. We need to be awake, judging the good and bad *within ourselves* with discernment and vigour, mending our ways but also trusting with confidence that God's love and forgiveness are available to us. We must not sleepwalk through our lives. And second, that the seat of *judgement over others* is never ours to sit on. Never. Jesus puts this directly in the sermon on the mount and elsewhere: do not judge, so that you may not be judged; first take the log out of your own eye; forgive one another without limit.

In the harvest parable quoted above from Matthew, Jesus makes the same point in a different way. In this life, the good and the bad must grow together. Judgement is reserved to the divine realm at the end of time. For us to take that part now is tantamount to blasphemy. The only teeth about whose gnashing God invites us to muse are our own.

The following story borrows from John 8: 2-11 but is fictitious.

It was early on the day of judgement, and some angels brought to Jesus a man who had been caught judging other people. They asked whether they should cast him into the furnace of fire. Jesus bent down and wrote with his finger on the ground. After a while Jesus heard deep weeping and gnashing of teeth, and he looked up. Of the angels there was no longer any sign. Jesus said to the man, 'Has no one condemned you?' The shaking of his teeth made it hard to hear the man's reply. Then Jesus said, 'Neither do I condemn you. Go and do not judge again.'

AUTUMN STORMS

October is a time which can see natural storms, sometimes destructive and terrifying, mark the change of seasons from summer towards winter. In modern society we may be as badly affected by economic storms of which October has had a share too. The infamous Wall Street Crash took place on 29 October 1929, and 1987 combined a natural storm and an economic storm.

The Gospels credit Jesus with the ability to still storms. But the message which in so doing he left with his disciples was about his divine nature, sharing God's power above all storms, and not a transferable skill.

As we face storms (natural and economic) we may feel closer to Job, the writer in the Old Testament upon whom disaster after disaster unjustly fell, and who challenged God to face him directly to account for the injustice. Four people, in the guise perhaps of messengers, attempt unsuccessfully to defend God's position in human terms. Then God responds to Job directly. He affirms Job's integrity and restores to him long life, wealth and a happy and multiplied family. But in terms of the question asked, God's answer seems to be that there are questions beyond human understanding, and this is one of them. In any event, of the fact that storms are part of the plan God leaves no doubt.

Job 38: 4–7, 16-18, 22-27, 34-36
Then the Lord answered Job out of the whirlwind: Where were you when I laid the foundation of the earth? Tell me, if you have understanding. Who determined its measurements – surely you know! Or who stretched the line upon it? On what were its bases sunk, or who laid its cornerstone when the morning stars sang together and all the heavenly beings shouted for joy?

Have you entered into the springs of the sea, or walked in the recesses of the deep? Have the gates of death been revealed to you, or have you seen the gates of deep darkness? Have you comprehended the expanse of the earth? Declare, if you know all this.

Have you entered the storehouses of the snow, or have you seen the storehouses of the hail, which I have reserved for the time of trouble, for the day of battle and war? What is the way to the place where the light is distributed, or where the east wind is scattered upon the earth?

Who has cut a channel for the torrents of rain, and a way for the thunderbolt, to bring rain on a land where no one lives, on the desert which is empty of human life, to satisfy the waste and desolate land, and to make the ground put forth grass?

Can you lift up your voice to the clouds, so that a flood of waters may cover you? Can you send forth lightnings, so that they may go and say to you, 'Here we are'?

Who has put wisdom in the inward parts, or given understanding to the mind?

Merciful Lord
We pray for a world which faces economic storms.
We think of parts of our world which also face unfair trade
barriers and have weakened financial and social systems.
We pray for industries and regions which face decline.
We pray for those who seek to overcome these problems globally,
nationally and locally.
Make us attentive to the consequences of our own behaviour as
employees, consumers, shareholders and voters.
In Jesus' name we ask.

God of storms
You have entered into the springs of the sea and walked in the recesses of the deep. You have stood in our skin, felt our fear and experienced our blindness.
Make the coming storm gentle, if it can be.
Make us courageous, if we can be.
But above all make us humble before you.
In Jesus' name we ask.

CHRISTMAS SHOPPING

A consequence in modern times of there being only fifty-four days between the end of October and the arrival of Christmas is that there are only fifty-four shopping days between the end of October and Christmas. No similar limit applies to the number of times during this season when you may be asked to enjoy, for example, 'Rocking Around The Christmas Tree'.

This second poem from the group at St Martin's which encourages people who are homeless to express themselves in creative writing comes from 'Smelling It Straight – Writing from St Martin-in-the-Fields 2001'. Like the first poem (reproduced at the end of January for Homelessness Sunday) this poem is not religious, or a prayer. It does describe piercingly, through its author's vision, part of the landscape of our society.

NINE DAYS OF CHRISTMAS

On the first day of Christmas my true love said to me:
'Get a job and some money for the kids and me!'

On the second day of Christmas my true love said to me:
'Two Raleigh bikes and some money for the kids and me.'

On the third day of Christmas my true love said to me:
'Three roast turkeys, two Raleigh bikes and some money for the kids and me.'

On the fourth day of Christmas my true love said to me:
'Four playstations, three roast turkeys, two Raleigh bikes and some money for the kids and me.'

On the fifth day of Christmas my true love said to me:
'Five mobile phones, four playstations, three roast turkeys, two
Raleigh bikes and some money for the kids and me.'

On the sixth day of Christmas my true love said to me:
'Six table and chairs, five mobile phones, four playstations, three
roast turkeys, two Raleigh bikes and some money for the kids and
me.'

On the seventh day of Christmas my true love said to me:
'Seven Bond videos, six table and chairs, five mobile phones, four
playstations, three roast turkeys, two Raleigh bikes and some
money for the kids and me.'

On the eighth day of Christmas my true love said to me:
'Eight telly tubbies, seven Bond videos, six table and chairs, five
mobile phones, four playstations, three roast turkeys, two Raleigh
bikes and some money for the kids and me.'

On the ninth day of Christmas I said to my true love:
'I'm divorcing you.'

Chris Spink

ALL SAINTS' DAY

(1 November)

All Saints' Day, preceded by the creepiness of Hallowe'en, holds together as one community the living and the dead. Together they expose the limited range of images that we hold in common with which to explore what (if anything) eternal life might mean.

Perhaps in our time when we bury or cremate people we should put with them their credit cards. A credit card statement can evoke rather well the modern paradigms by which we interpret existence.

For example, we experience life and death schizophrenically. Sometimes the way existence feels to us is that we are unique and precious. Equally it may make us feel statistically insignificant. So with a credit card. Our own card is a unique and precious thing which we take care not to lose, yet at the same time (even if it has an endangered whale on it) we know it is exactly like millions of others.

More profoundly, most of us understand life as a straight-line sequence of events in time with linked cause and accountability, which is what a credit card statement is. What I have done in the past adds up to alter what I can do in the future. If I make only the minimum repayment this month, I will be affected next month. This time-line experience of life and identity appears to be encoded powerfully within us.

A consequence is that what we are most likely to think eternal life might be is a special platinum card existence, with no expiry date and possibly some sort of moral balance transfer from this life. To this we may add some uncertainty as to whether there will be nice enough things to buy in heaven when we get there. This picture of what eternal life might be may have power over us whether we say we believe in eternal life or not.

This picture or one like it is also common to the many everyday jokes in which the Christian heaven is "boring". But what other pictures do we have? If we try to visualise eternal life as Hollywood would have it ('Your Life: The Sequel'), then it is true that the "heaven" section of The Bible Video and DVD Shop has a limited range to offer. The directors are heavily reliant upon mountain scenes, possibly sponsored by a manufacturer of laundry detergent (the *radiance* of those clothes!). How different in Islam – the "heaven" shelves are overflowing with vivid action movies.

The problem is that the time-line model of heaven does not work, and this tests to the limit (and probably beyond) our capacity to imagine really critical things like relationships within a heaven. For example the challenge which the Sadducees, who did not believe in heaven, put to Jesus concerning a woman who ends up having married a succession of seven brothers: 'In the resurrection whose wife will she be?' (Mark 12: 18-25). Jesus' answer ('When they rise from the dead, they neither marry nor are given in marriage, but are like angels in heaven') only takes us so far.

What kind of relatedness can one picture which would survive the Sadducee test – *any* kind? If none, the sense in which there can be any meaningful connection between my earthly identity and any hypothetical heavenly identity seems dangerously small.

A different image would be one of heaven as a forest of large trees. Trees with giant, interlocking root systems. Each root system, unique to each tree like a fingerprint, represents a pattern of desires, refined, exposed and matured through our human journey.

Imagine "desires" here in the largest possible sense, to include desires for peace or for justice, as well as for art or for music – or for other people. Parents with young children typically find that even the smallest infant has a different pattern of desires from his or her siblings.

If this pattern identifies us and connects us together, then it also provides a means to identify others to whom we are close (ie we understand their desires deeply), for we can recognise within the forest the patterns of what they desire. It also enables mutual connection (if we desire each other then our root systems interlock). And of course to belong to the forest at all is only possible if one desires to be in the presence of the One, whose own desire Jesus describes thus:

John 17: 22-24
The glory that you have given me I have given them, so that they may be one, as we are one, I in them and you in me, that they may become completely one, so that the world may know that you have sent me and have loved them even as you have loved me. Father, I desire that those also, whom you have given me, may be with me where I am, to see my glory, which you have given me because you loved me before the foundation of the world.

FUNERALS AND BEREAVEMENT

However it may be in heaven, death shatters our interconnectedness here. If death propels us anywhere, to human understanding that place is a void, and dark.

John Donne's *No man is an island* (1624) is captured in music and language of a different era by the American singer and songwriter Jackson Browne in his song *For A Dancer* (1974). The lyrics express the interconnectedness and as well as the separatedness which define modern life and death. In hinting at the possibility, but likely unreachability, of meaning they also speak of our times.

There is nothing about our times which makes them wise times, right times. By grace we may face the beyond and say, with St Paul and without pretence:

(Romans 8: 38-39; 1 Corinthians 15: 19)
neither death, nor life, nor angels, nor rulers, nor things present, nor things to come, nor powers, nor height, nor depth, nor anything else in all creation will be able to separate us from the love of God in Christ Jesus our Lord … If for this life only we have hoped in Christ, we are of all people most to be pitied.

But Christians are not called to be islands; the images Jesus used were light and salt. Even if we have that kind of faith which does not know doubt, we all love and grieve for many people whose understanding of life and death is much closer to Jackson Browne's slightly confused, slightly contradictory song than to St Paul's. And that faith is also faith which, while not overcome by doubt, finds that doubt and pain have moved in with suitcases. That is the faith of the final prayer in this section.

The Naked Year

FOR A DANCER

Keep a fire burning in your eye
Pay attention to the open sky
You never know what will be coming down
I don't remember losing track of you
You were always dancing in and out of view
I must have thought you'd always be around
Always keeping things real by playing the clown
Now you're nowhere to be found

I don't know what happens when people die
Can't seem to grasp it as hard as I try
It's like a song I can hear playing right in my ear
That I can't sing
I can't help listening

And I can't help feeling stupid standing 'round
Crying as they ease you down
'Cause I know that you'd rather we were dancing
Dancing our sorrow away
No matter what fate chooses to play
There's nothing you can do about it anyway

Just do the steps that you've been shown
By everyone you've ever known
Until the dance becomes your very own
No matter how close to yours
Another's steps have grown
In the end there is one dance you'll do alone

Keep a fire for the human race
Let your prayers go drifting into space
You never know what will be coming down
Perhaps a better world is drawing near
And just as easily it could all disappear

Along with whatever meaning you might have found
Don't let the uncertainty turn you around
The world keeps turning around and around
Go on and make a joyful sound

Into a dancer you have grown
From a seed somebody else has thrown
Go on ahead and throw some seeds of your own
And somewhere between the time you arrive
And the time you go
May lie a reason you were alive
But you'll never know

Jackson Browne

A PRAYER OF BEREAVEMENT

Almighty God
You have spun our lives like gossamer between the stars
Each strand held in your hands.
You show us that you love us
And tell us death is not the end.

But this morning
The mirror looked at my cracked face
And the cold sink winced under my raging hands
Until the plughole confessed
That my life had been poured away yesterday.

So I shan't do astral gossamer today, if that's all right with you.
Don't paint Death's face in too friendly a light
Or I might start wondering about the two of you.

But for your help
In Jesus' name I ask.

FRIENDSHIP

(Guy Fawkes' Day, 5 November)

People have their days of birth and death, marriages have their anniversaries, romance has St Valentine's Day, mothers and fathers have Mothers' and Fathers' days. But friendship, though compellingly precious to everyone, is homeless. My reasons for choosing Guy Fawkes' Day (marking his betrayal and arrest on 5 November 1605 for the Gunpowder Plot to blow up Parliament) have everything to do with me and nothing to do with him! Your own associations with friendship will of course be quite different.

Friendship is given in many kinds, in contrasting depths, textures and sizes. Sometimes its cloth is woven over decades of shared experience. The grace below grew out of that kind of friendship. It was written for the celebration at Hever Castle in 2002 of the fiftieth birthday of my friend and business partner, Stephen Bampfylde. But sometimes friendship is given briefly, but nevertheless profoundly, by people whose names and lives we do not know.

I grew up in Hong Kong and my family remained there when I came to boarding school in London from my fifteenth birthday. That was a somewhat strange experience, at times lonely. Among the hazards to be survived were half-terms (an odd concept to me) when, if not looked after by relations, I stayed with families who were paid to look after me.

Though I have never remembered the name of my friend, I will never forget one half-term Saturday night, which happened to be when the bonfires of Guy Fawkes were burning. The son of my hosts took me to see the bonfire and fireworks. Afterwards he showed me how buying a pint in a pub works. The definition of banality? Quite the opposite for me.

A GRACE FOR LOVE, FRIENDSHIP AND LIFE

Heavenly Father
We spend much of our time and energy as if we were creatures of ambition, achievement and calculation.
But you spread before us this banquet of life – a banquet of love beyond reason, friendship beyond price and life itself beyond our control.
However many times it may be said of each one of us that we were truly grateful, may this occasion be one of them.

THE FALL OF THE BERLIN WALL

(9 November 1989)

A reflection, and a prayer, about freedom.

A tiny reminder of the relationship between faiths such as Christianity and freedom comes in George Orwell's *Nineteen Eighty-Four*, in the scene in which the central character (Winston) stumbles across the upper room with a beautiful mahogany bed and, he believes, no all-seeing telescreen. He is shown the room by the kindly old antique shop owner, Charrington, who tells him that the print fixed to the wall is of a now-ruined church, St Clement Dane's. Charrington recalls the nursery rhyme

"Oranges and lemons, say the bells of St Clement's
You owe me three farthings, say the bells of St Martin's —'
there, now that's as far as I can get. A farthing, that was a small copper
coin, looked something like a cent.'

'Where was St Martin's?' said Winston.

'St Martin's? That's still standing. It's in Victory Square, alongside the
picture gallery. A building with a kind of a triangular porch and pillars in
front, and a big flight of steps.'

Winston knew the place well. It was a museum used for propaganda
displays of various kinds – scale models of rocket bombs and Floating
Fortresses, waxwork tableaux illustrating enemy atrocities, and the like.

It is the room in which Winston and Julia are arrested by Charrington, who turns out to be a member of the thought police. The telescreen was concealed behind the picture.

Freedom is such a fundamental part of what makes our life and our faith possible that we risk overlooking it. Christians in several other countries (or for that matter several books in both the Old and New Testaments) could correct us.

When 1984 came around, one of the most powerful symbols of lack of freedom was the Berlin Wall. By then the 100 km Wall was in its fourth generation of design and construction. It incorporated the "'death strip", a strip of land between six metres and fifteen metres wide with five metre high light masts, in which the East German shoot-to-kill policy was enforced vigorously until 3 April 1989.

The "fall" of the Wall on 9 November 1989 was an astonishing moment for freedom in Europe. How the Wall was put up, and how it fell, are like reflecting mirrors which capture between them the struggle between freedom and control. The story is told fully in *Divided City – The Berlin Wall*.

The night of 12 August 1961 was a mild summer night in a tranquil Berlin, and the first hour of 13 August was no different. At 1.10 am East Berlin radio interrupted its *Melodies at Night* programme with an announcement that the Warsaw Pact governments had approached East Germany 'with the suggestion that measures be taken at the border to effectively remove the subversive activities directed against the countries of the socialist bloc and to secure reliable surveillance of the entire territory of West Berlin.' At 1.54 am train service across the city's border stopped without warning.

By 2.20 am the reports coming in to West Berlin police headquarters were grim: 'Fifteen military trucks with Vopos (People's Police) at the Oberbaum Bridge.' 'Armoured scout cars at Sonnenallee.' 'Hundreds of Vopos and border guards armed with machine guns at Brandenburg Gate.' 8,000 East German soldiers were deployed with tanks. By 3.53 am the German press agency reported, 'Vopo putting up barbed wire.' The Wall had begun, unveiled at night in a ruthlessly effective display of planning and discipline.

It fell in a collapse of the same qualities of planning and control which had given it birth. On 4 November 1989, almost half a million East Berliners had gathered at Alexanderplatz to demand free elections and freedom to travel. The East German Government reformed itself on 7 November, and an international press conference was held on the evening of 9 November. At 6.53 pm the party spokesman Günter Schabowski was handed a piece of paper and announced that travel restrictions across the East German border were to be relaxed. Immediately the journalists asked, 'Does this apply to West Berlin as well?' Schabowski was at a loss and fumbled in his papers. 'Well (pause) – yes, yes.'

'When does this take effect?' Making up an answer, Schabowski said 'To my knowledge, it is to take effect immediately, without delay.'

By 8.30 pm crowds were assembling at the Wall crossing points, and growing rapidly. The border guards were unable to obtain instructions from their headquarters and ministries. At Bornholmer Strasse, the checkpoint supervisor First Lieutenant Jäger was unable to obtain instructions from the State Security Service. At 10.30pm, facing a tumultuous crowd and fearing for the lives of the guards, he took his own initiative and opened the border. By midnight people were pouring freely eastwards and westwards across all the crossing points, ecstatic, searching for relations and family.

For a while the East German soldiers deployed water cannon, hosing down border violators and aiming at people on the Wall.

But freedom would not be drenched. Eventually the soldiers stopped and took off their helmets. People came down from the wall – they talked to the guards – they shared cigarettes – they were ecstatic. And they were, in a new way, free.

If the central ethical teaching of Christianity is to love your neighbour as yourself, its central teaching about God is that He hungers and dies and rises to lead us out of slavery. The first covenant is made with the Jews on their journey of faith out of slavery. They commemorate this journey in the Passover. Jesus is killed at the Passover and institutes the Eucharist, a new Passover meal which celebrates our God-won freedom. For St Paul, this was freedom from the slavery of sin and death. For the writer of John's Gospel, 'you will know the truth, and the truth will make you free' (John 8: 32).

For us, from what shall we choose to be free?

Almighty God
Freedom is your self-revealing gift, offered to all in creation.
Through Jesus you invite us to make that place our home
where freedom lives in the divine heart.
Awake us from our dreams to celebrate our freedom
Teach us how to use freedom
Strengthen us to defend it
And hand victory to all those who are denied it.
In Jesus' name we ask.

REMEMBRANCE SUNDAY

(The Sunday nearest Armistice Day and St Martin's Day, 11 November)

St Martin, soldier and bishop, is patron saint of soldiers and pacifists. The quotation at the end of these prayers comes from Martin Luther King. These prayers were prayed at St Martin-in-the-Fields on 12 November 2000.

A LITANY OF REMEMBRANCE FOR A CENTURY OF WAR

1 August 1914, Lieutenant Henri Desagneaux.
'At last in the afternoon I catch the first train which comes along. The compartments are bursting at the seams with people from all classes of society. At level crossings, in the towns, crowds singing *La Marseillaise* gather to greet the troops. The general impression is the following: it's Kaiser Bill who wanted war, it had to happen and we shall never have such a fine opportunity again.' *Father forgive us, for we know not what we do.*

11 November 1918, David Lloyd George, prime minister.
'At eleven o'clock this morning came to an end the cruellest and most terrible war that has ever scourged mankind. I hope we may say that thus, this fateful morning, came to an end all wars.'

30 September 1938, Neville Chamberlain, prime minister.
'This is the second time in our history that there has come back from Germany to Downing Street peace with honour. I believe it is peace for our time.' *Father forgive us, for we know not what we do.*

---

20 January 1942, Reinhard Heydrich, Wannsee.
'It is the Reichsführer's will that the Jewish question is settled ... in one clean sweep. The total Jews concerned – 11 million.'

4 September 1942, Chaim Rumkowski, addressing the Jewish ghetto in Lodz.
'I must tell you a secret: they requested 24,000 victims, 3,000 a day for eight days. I succeeded in reducing the number to 20,000; but only on condition that these would be children below the age of ten.' *Father forgive us, for we know not what we do.*

16 July 1945, in the New Mexico desert, physicist Robert Oppenheimer.
'I remembered the line from the Hindu scripture, the Bhagavad Gita: I am become death, the destroyer of worlds.'

3 October 1957, at the Labour Party conference, Aneurin Bevan.
'You call that statesmanship? I call it an emotional spasm ... I do seriously believe in the rejection of the bomb. But if resolution twenty-four is read with its implications, it means that as decent folk you must immediately repudiate all the protection and all the alliances and all the entanglements you have with anybody who uses or possesses or manufactures hydrogen bombs. I find it a very, very serious dilemma.' *Father forgive us, for we know not what we do.*

30 January 1972, in Derry, a nineteen year old member of the ambulance corps.
'There was one man what wanted to try and get across. He stepped out and a soldier came round the corner of the Rossville Street flats. The man raised his hand in the air – right out – and shouted 'Don't shoot, don't shoot'. Seconds later he was just shot in the head.'

26 July 1982, Archbishop Robert Runcie.
'In our prayers we shall quite rightly remember those who are bereaved in our own country and the relations of the young Argentinian soldiers who were killed ... A shared anguish can be a bridge of reconciliation. Our neighbours are indeed like us.'

11 July 1995, in Srebrenica, General Radislav Krstic.
'Here we are on the eve of yet another great Serb holiday. Finally it has come, to take revenge on the Turks.' *Father forgive us, for we know not what we do.*

Heavenly Father, you gave us a Martin for our century. He said:
'One day youngsters will learn words they will not understand.
Children from India will ask: what is hunger?
Children from Alabama will ask: what is racial segregation?
Children from Hiroshima will ask: what is the atomic bomb?
Children at school will ask: what is war?

'You will answer them. You will tell them:
These words are not used any more.
Like stage-coaches, galleys or slavery: words no longer meaningful.
That is why they have been removed from dictionaries.'

Heavenly Father, in giving us this Martin's hope, give us also his courage;
the same hope and courage as of unnumbered slaughtered millions whom we now remember,
and bring us with them home at last.
In Jesus' name we ask.

CHRIST THE KING

(Sunday between 20 and 26 November)

The festival of Christ the King calls to mind the question posed at Epiphany, when the infant Jesus receives the homage of those who had travelled from a distant country. What king is this, whose kingship is asserted over you and me, and what kind of kingdom? Before whom, and why, shall I kneel?

We are people suspicious of extraordinary power, and with reason. An icon for our times was the lone student in front of the tanks in Tienanmen Square. People suspicious of power are bound to be people suspicious of God.

Arguably Jesus only taught on one theme – the nature of the kingdom, the kingship, and the power of heaven. From the sermon on the mount to the healing of the sick, from the wedding feast to the woman caught in adultery, from playing with children to dying on the cross, nothing else seemed as important to him. It was not the kingship that people expected – or perhaps wanted. The student in front of the tanks wants a power which will overcome the tanks; instead Christ kneels to wash his feet. (Except this is not 'instead': *this is the power* says the Christ, and it *will overcome* the tanks.)

So we kneel because he knelt first, to wash our feet. To show us respect. To say we are worth it. Including the one who will betray him. That is the human level of the interaction.

And if we kneel before the man, we may or may not see
something more. We may see who the man is. 'Autumn Storms'
quoted the rejoinder of God to the righteous Job, who questioned
God's morality. Where were you when I laid the foundation of the
earth? Are you my equal? Job answers, see I am of small account,
what shall I answer you? But Jesus answers, *before Abraham was, I am*
(Job 38: 4, 40: 4 and John 8: 58).

Henri Nouwen sees a different aspect of God in a famous picture
of someone kneeling before a figure of authority – Rembrandt's
'The Return of the Prodigal Son'. The younger son who has
returned kneels, ragged, in front of his aged father clad in a broad
red cloak. Other figures look on. In the final part of his book of
the same title, Nouwen sees motherly as well as fatherly elements
in this painting of the kingdom of heaven, and writes (pp 100-
102):

*As I now look again at Rembrandt's old man bending over his returning
son and touching his shoulders with his hands, I begin to see not only a
father who 'clasps his son in his arms', but also a mother who caresses her
child, surrounds him with the warmth of her body and holds him against
the womb from which he sprang. Thus the 'return of the prodigal son'
becomes the return to God's womb, the return to the very origins of
being…*

*Now I understand better also the enormous stillness of this portrait of God.
There is no sentimentality here, no romanticism, no simplistic tale with a
happy ending. What I see here is God as mother, receiving back into her
womb the one whom she made in her own image. The near-blind eyes, the
hands, the cloak, the bent-over body, they all call forth the divine maternal
love, marked by grief, desire, hope and endless waiting.*

*The mystery, indeed, is that God in her infinite compassion has linked
herself for eternity with the life of her children. She has freely chosen to*

become dependent on her creatures, whom she has gifted with freedom. This choice causes her grief when they leave; this choice brings her gladness when they return. But her joy will not be complete until all who have received life from her have returned home and gather round the table prepared for them.

Reproduced with permission of Darton, Longman and Todd Ltd)

ADVENT SUNDAY

(Sunday between 27 November and 3 December)

Advent calls us to prepare for the coming of Christ into the world.

Since the arrival of psychology in the nineteenth century, critics of religion have employed the concept of psychological projection to criticise our tendency to form images of god(s) which are – they argue – parts of ourselves misleadingly externalised. For example (Peter Singer writing about Hegel, p 84):

'Hegel's target is any religion which divides human nature against itself – and he asserts that this is the upshot of any religion which separates man from God, putting God in a "beyond" outside the human world. This conception of God, he maintains, is really a projection of one aspect of human nature. What the unhappy consciousness does not realise is that the spiritual qualities of God which it worships are in fact qualities of its own self. It is in this sense that the unhappy consciousness is an alienated soul: it has projected its own essential nature into a place forever out of its reach, and one which makes the real world in which it lives seem, by contrast, miserable and insignificant.'

(Reproduced with permission of Oxford University Press)

The bursting of an incarnate God *into this world,* affirming this life as the opposite of miserable and insignificant, argues against this characterisation of religion. But, equipped with the insights of psychology, we should take some care that the God whom we welcome at Christmas is indeed God, utterly Other, and not a projection. One of the Biblical God's most frequent injunctions in the Old Testament is to abjure the worship of manufactured gods, such as carved images. These days we do the carving in our minds.

The classical Advent images of preparation for the incarnation are of darkness and of watchfulness; of waiting for the light of God's revelation. In many churches an additional candle is lit each week during this season, marking the approach of Christmas. A different way of marking Advent would be to put out candles, increasing the darkness as Christmas (closely following the northern hemisphere's longest night) approaches. For the candles can represent our inadequate, and partly projected, symbols and conceptions of God. We can put them out to make ready for a new birth: the arrival of One who cannot be captured by our preconceptions.

Almighty God
You created the first darkness as well as the first light.
Help us make ready for your arrival
by emptying ourselves of fixed images
and by putting out familiar lights.
So may we with more open eyes and greater joy
receive you into our lives this Christmas.

IMAGINE

(the assassination of John Lennon, 8 December 1980)

There are few modern songs to rival *Imagine*, and very few to achieve its anthemic quality. In just the first 24 words, written on a hotel bill and then harmonised on an all-white piano in an all-white room, John Lennon has already made it possible to imagine that religion is a principal cause of the world's pain. Was he right?

The resonance of the words of *Imagine* stand comparison with the Sermon on the Mount, with no contest as to which could be recited from memory by more people. The song asks us to imagine no heaven, no hell, no countries, no religion and no possessions, with the dreamt-for result that everyone lives in peace, for today and as one.

Yet Lennon ushered the song into the world as a fantasy, not a creed. No possessions was not meant to suggest that he or Yoko Ono would give up any of their five apartments in the Dakota building in New York. Consider the word "sincerity" when Ray Coleman writes in his biography of Lennon (p 580):

'Such was the intrinsic beauty of the song and the sincerity with which Lennon sang it that it will stand forever as an international anthem. All Lennon was asking was that we should *imagine* a world without possessions or religion.'

Coleman means us to understand by "sincerity" something beautiful – the unforcedness of a beautiful dream – but something quite different from the sincerity (or otherwise) of Gandhi, Martin Luther King or Jesus Christ. The Sermon on the Mount did not say *imagine* how nice it would be if peacemakers were blessed. Indeed preserving a roguishness, a lack of seriousness, was important to Lennon:

'So I refuse to lead, and I'll always show my genitals or something which prevents me from being Martin Luther King or Gandhi, and getting killed' (quoted by Jack Jones in *Let Me Take You Down*, p261).

It did not work. Sometime after 5 pm on 8 December 1980 on the pavement of West 72nd Street outside the Dakota building, beneath dim incandescent street lamps and the all-white room where *Imagine* was born, a fan who had travelled from Hawaii got his hero's autograph on the new Double Fantasy album. 'Is that all you want?' Lennon asked. Unfortunately it was not. At 10.50 pm that evening, clutching the album and a copy of J D Salinger's *The Catcher in the Rye*, Mark Chapman shot Lennon in the back five times and killed him. Chapman then waited to be caught.

The psychiatric determination on Chapman was that he was fit to stand trial. Jack Jones' book traced Chapman's story with care.

The web of connection between Chapman and Lennon has many strands – including religion, drugs (the Beatles' 'Magical Mystery Tour' introduced Chapman to them) and the plot of Salinger's book. But the thickest strand was rage at betrayal: betrayal of a faith that Chapman had invested in Lennon, notwithstanding Lennon's perception of his own trade as fantasy, not faith. Chapman recalls finding a book on Lennon in the Honolulu public library (Jones, pp 219-220):

'I remember thinking that there was a successful man who had the world on a chain. And there I was not even a link of that chain. Just a person who had no personality. A walking void who had given a great deal of my

*time and thoughts and energy into what John Lennon had said and had
sung about and had done – and had told all of us to do – in the sixties
and early seventies, when I was growing up, when I was first trying to
make sense out of a world that was so painful and hurtful and sad.*

*'I checked out the book and brought it home to my wife and pointed out
the pictures to her, pictures of him smiling on the roof of the sumptuous
Dakota building: the decadent bastard, the phoney bastard, who had lied to
children, who had used his music to mislead a generation of people who
desperately needed to believe in love and a world at war that desperately
needed to believe in peace.*

*'He told us to imagine no possessions, and there he was, with millions of
dollars and yachts and farms and country estates, laughing at people like
me who had believed the lies and bought the records and built a big part of
our lives around his music.'*

Lennon said "Imagine", and Chapman did – he dreamt the dream.
The dream of the song is a universal dream, found even within
religion – for example in Revelation 21, where the Christian
vision of the new Jerusalem is of a city beyond possessions and
national strife and without a temple, for religion will have passed
away.

The ending of religion and the abolition of violence are both holy
dreams. But we will sail to neither place on the sea of fantasy.

———————

Lord Jesus Christ
You spent your time with visionaries and criminals alike.
Like visionaries and criminals we try in our own ways
to make sense of a world which can be so painful and hurtful and sad.
Heal us and forgive us, especially when the world makes no sense.
Into that world make us channels of your grace.
Give us, not the dream of peace, but the reality of forgiveness;
Not fantasy, but commitment to others;
Not imagination, but hope.
In your name we ask.

The lyrics of *Imagine* can be found at many websites,
for example *www.merseyworld.com/imagine*

CHRISTMAS EVE

(24 December)

God our father and mother
Your Christmas eyes see children;
and people who have forgotten how to be children;
and some people who never knew.
Your arms reach out and hold all of us.

Children are so close to you:
so open about what they want
trusting from birth in the possibility of joy.

So in the middle of crowds and of togetherness
Surrounded by music, laughter and food lovingly prepared
Give us an experience of the Christmas feast, with heaven and
earth dancing together.
Give us trust once again in the possibility of joy.
Give us the gifts of childhood.

In Jesus' name we ask.

CHRISTMAS

(25 December)

The celebration of the birth of Jesus at Bethlehem.

Put the presents outside, would you, and ask the shepherds to wait in the hall? Did you say there are already angels in the living room? Then be a darling and ask the rest of the heavenly choir if they wouldn't mind waiting in the kitchen. Quite right, if the shepherds are with their flocks, the porch would be better. No, I don't remember when the wise men said they would get here, but if they really are wise men it won't be for quite a while. Now – where were we?

Pull the Christian cracker apart and what falls out is you, God and a baby. The existence of God has had a bumpy ride. Occasionally so has the existence of the baby. But the existence of *you* has seemed safe – good old Descartes, you think, therefore you are! That god-like self-certainty of existence: enjoy the feeling, since we may be the last human generation able to do so.

Professor of cognitive studies and polymath Daniel Dennett argues that the obvious intuitions which we typically have about selves in general and ourself in particular do not stand up well to logical analysis and the advances in his science. In his language, selves turn out to be fictions. We posit a narrator – we hypothesise an 'I' – at the centre of our world and rationalise confusing events into a narrative because it is a powerful idea which works – especially in an environment hugely dominated by words and ideas.

What is an 'I', if Dennett is right? He writes (*Consciousness Explained*, pp 429-430):

Think of Ishmael, in Moby Dick. 'Call me Ishmael' is the way the text opens, and we oblige. We don't call the text Ishmael, and we don't call Melville [the author] Ishmael. Who or what do we call Ishmael? We call Ishmael Ishmael, the wonderful fictional character to be found in the pages of Moby Dick. 'Call me Dan,' you hear from my lips, and you oblige, not by calling my lips Dan, or my body Dan, but by calling me Dan, the theorists' fiction created by – well, not by me but by my brain, acting in concert over the years with my parents and siblings and friends …

But don't I exist?

Of course you do. There you are, sitting in the chair, reading my book and raising challenges. And curiously enough, your current embodiment, though a necessary precondition for your creation, is not necessarily a requirement for your existence to be prolonged indefinitely … your existence depends on the persistence of that narrative (rather like the Thousand and One Arabian Nights, but all a single tale) which could theoretically survive indefinitely many switches of medium, be teleported as readily (in principle) as the evening news, and stored indefinitely as sheer information.

(Reproduced with permission of Penguin Press)

It is a delicious levelling of the playing field, as we enter the twenty-first century, to glimpse that exactly the same reasoning applies to the personhood or not of any of the three bits which fall out of the Christian Christmas cracker. Any baby has to learn to treat himself or herself as a person. The baby may then learn to treat you as a person. As for God, who shall say? The only way to be a person is to have a name and tell a story ('Call me Ishmael').

In the burning bush, God responds to Moses' request for the divine name with 'I am' (Exodus 3: 14). To claim to be an "I" is to claim to be a person. And the story about God which we are told through the opening of John's Gospel is one which sits quite comfortably in the world visualised by Daniel Dennett two millennia later:

(John 1: 1-5, 14)
In the beginning was the Word, and the Word was with God, and the Word was God. He was in the beginning with God. All things came into being through him, and without him not one thing came into being. What has come into being in him was life, and the life was the light of all people. The light shines in the darkness, and the darkness did not overcome it.

And the Word became flesh and lived among us, and we have seen his glory, the glory as of a father's only son, full of grace and truth.

BOXING DAY

(26 December)

Christmas comes at a time of tremendous make-believe and bingeing. At the time of the shortest day we make-believe with coloured lights, alcohol or airplane tickets that winter does not have us under its lash. We binge, if we can get them, on food and drink and old movies and things of all kinds. And we binge on family. The two reflections here are about spiritual moderation and about the reality of family.

The language and thought of Christianity (or how we have
received these things) easily give prominence to an all-or-nothing
view of the world and of the spiritual journey. Think of the many
hellfire sermons, or the message in Revelation 3: 15-16 to the early
Christians at Laodicea: 'I know your works; you are neither cold
nor hot. I wish that you were either cold or hot. So, because you
are lukewarm, and neither cold nor hot, I am about to spit you out
my mouth.'

Perhaps certain frames of thought naturally "favour" certain tones
of voice, just as certain building architectures bring out the best in
different music and singing. It is not that other voices are not there,
rather that they may be more easily missed – for instance within
Christianity the doubting of the apostle Thomas, the not-yetness of
St Augustine or, thus far, the many voices of women.

This means that one of the blessings which different religions can
offer each other is not simply to engage intellectually with what is
said – although that is one valid form of engagement. In addition,
we can listen with a different purpose and different results to the
tones of voice which come through more strongly in other
people's religions than in our own; that we might become more
sensitive to the voices within our own tradition which may get lost
in our religion's architecture.

For example, Tenzin Gyatso, His Holiness the Dalai Lama, teaches
about materialism that it is not bad for someone to have as much
they want, if others also have as much they want and need. He
notes the potential contradiction that if he is staying in a hotel in
an international city and sees a workers' demonstration going by,

he is drawn to join in – yet he is the one enjoying the comforts of the hotel. He says:

'I do not believe everyone can or should be like Mahatma Gandhi and live the life of a poor peasant. Such dedication is wonderful and greatly to be admired. But the watchword is 'As much as we can' – without going to extremes' (Ancient Wisdom, Modern World, p 184).

Considering his elucidation of the issues could help Christians do two things. It could stimulate a deeper and clearer engagement with what Christian understandings of materialism and poverty are, and what understanding we shall make our own. And hearing a different voice could also make us more thoughtful about the possibility that the all-or-nothing voice within Christianity drowns out the other God-given voices which are also there.

On families

One of the things on which it is traditional to binge at Christmas is families and relations. One of the things which can make Christmas acutely painful for some people with families, as well as for many people without, is the degree of make-believe about the goodness and completeness of families. In reality, life in and around many families is like life in and around many people – enriching, complex and incomplete.

Just as families are incomplete, so are individual perspectives on them. Duwayne Brooks gives us his perspective on a friendship and two families, his own and Stephen Lawrence's, in chapter 2 of his book *Steve and Me*:

I know I was a difficult kid. Loyal and bright, but definitely stroppy. I don't suppose that I'm that different now. My mum found me difficult to cope with. She was strong and stroppy too.

My mum was one for laying down the law – a bit like Steve's mum. And one of her top laws was the washing-up law. The dishes were my responsibility. It shouldn't have been such a big deal, but it was … it would look like Mum had had a party and there'd be a huge pile of dishes blocking up the sink and trailing round the kitchen, and she wouldn't let me go to bed till they were all done.

One day when I was sixteen [in 1991], I was sitting in the house watching Manchester United on the telly, and Mum said would I do the dishes. I said, 'Yeah, I'll do them after the football.' Well, that was it, she exploded – said I could get out of the house right then. So I did.

I stayed at the first hostel in Sydenham for a month … it was so liberating after home. I just remember thinking to myself, Ah, peace and quiet, peace and quiet.

In 1992, from Stockwell I bounced temporarily out of the hostel system and into my gran's flat at Grove Park back in south-east London … It was at gran's that I hooked up with Mum again. She came round to see me, and, of course, she was hurt that I'd not been in touch … When I lived at home she didn't seem that interested in helping me, but now she came round and wanted to know if I needed anything – clothes, food, money.

Eventually I managed to move back closer to home … We'd [Steve and I] both grown up a bit. I'd found my own way to independence, and Steve was looking for his. He was brought up wrapped up in cotton wool. In a way, all the rules were just another aspect of this – they wanted the best for him, and they were strict with him so he couldn't mess things up. Then when he started doing stuff that they weren't so keen on, they became increasingly hard on him. He was smoking and drinking a bit, as were most boys his age. Like so many of our crowd, he was into the drink called

20/20. It's ironic really that his mum always warned him against me turning him to drink, when I couldn't stand the bloody stuff.

Steve asked what chance there would be of moving into the hostel. I said I'd look into it for him. But I never felt sure that he wanted to move out of home. He was torn — he was finding it impossible at home, but despite everything he didn't want to hurt his parents by walking out on them.

We saw a lot of each other that year. There was so much to catch up on, so much to talk about. We'd spend hours and hours just talking about nothing in the way that good friends do, arguing about football, arguing about girls, play-fighting, swapping stories, talking about the future, dreaming.

NEW YEAR'S EVE

(31 December)

Prayers adapted from those used at St Martin-in-the-Fields on the last Sunday of the millennium (26 December 1999).

In these final prayers of the year, let us look back to the beginning of the world and forward to the end of all things. We reflect with new intensity on the pilgrimage of our own life, lived out in God's perpetual "now".

The arrival of this millennium was greeted in London by the world's largest fireworks display. But in the real Big Bang, in the tiniest fraction of a second, you Lord created all matter, existence, time and causation, from which all life came to be. In the words of the astrophysicist and priest, Abbé George Lemaître:

'The evolution of the world may be compared to a display of fireworks that has just ended: some few red wisps, ashes and smoke. Standing on a cooled cinder, we see the slow fading of the suns, and we try to recall the vanished brilliance of the origin of the worlds.'

Eternal God, plant in our hearts a glimpse of the enormity of your power: power beyond imagining; power beyond thought; power beyond experience.
Blessed be God forever.

Against the magnificence of the heavens, we dwindle into specks. Against the pitilessness of scientific eternity, what is a human life, and a human lifetime?

Eternal God:
your power is rivalled only by your imagination;
your imagination by your humility;
your humility by your love;
and at this time of Christmas,
recalling your incarnation
we praise you with unbelievable joy.

You took on human life and declared to us, 'Just as you did it to one of the least of these who are members of my family, you did it to me.' You took on a human lifetime and, with bread and wine and nails and thorns, blessed it forever: this same time which we each experience:

'a time to be born and a time to die;
a time to plant and a time to pluck up what is planted;
a time to kill and a time to heal;
a time to break down and a time to build up;
a time to weep and a time to laugh;
a time to mourn and a time to dance;
a time to throw away stones and a time to gather stones together;
a time to embrace and a time to refrain from embracing;
a time to seek and a time to lose;
a time to keep and a time to throw away;
a time to tear and a time to sew;
a time to keep silence and a time to speak;
a time to love and a time to hate;
a time for war and a time for peace.'
Blessed be God forever.

Dare we look beyond our little span, to the next millennium?
Who knows what will stand here in a thousand years' time;
whether human life will still exist;
whether our successors, if we have successors,

---

will share this space with forms of life beyond our present knowledge.

What can we know of that world? We can know this:
that if Christianity still exists, this prayer will still be used;
and so we pray this way, affirming as we do our brotherhood and
sisterhood with generations past and generations to come, and with
Jesus Christ, God incarnate, who taught it to us:

Our Father in heaven
hallowed be your name
your kingdom come
your will be done
on earth as it is in heaven.
Give us today our daily bread.
Forgive us our sins
as we forgive those who sin against us.
Do not lead us into temptation
but deliver us from evil.
For the kingdom, the power and the glory are yours
Now and forever.
Amen.

The Biblical references are to Matthew 25: 40
and Ecclesiastes 3: 1-8.

The Naked Year

ACKNOWLEDGEMENTS AND SOURCES

I need to thank many people and am delighted to do so: for their nurture, support and inspiration the Rt Revd David Beetge, Bishop of the Highveld and Dean of the Anglican province of Southern Africa, and my wife Tricia Sibbons; for friendship and for giving time to my drafts as generously as if they were their own, Canon Geoffrey Brown, formerly Vicar of St Martin-in-the-Fields, Dr David Field, tutor at Oak Hill Theological College, the Revd Rosemary Lain-Priestley, Associate Vicar at St Martin's for the English-speaking congregations, and Rosemary Drew; and finally the Revd Nick Holtam, our present Vicar, and through him the whole community of faith at St Martin's. Directly and indirectly you have made possible what is here.

The sources below are gratefully acknowledged, including the generously given permission of many copyright holders. Every effort has been made to trace copyright holders where permission is required. Biblical quotations have been taken from the New Revised Standard Version of the Holy Bible, Anglicized Edition (Oxford University Press).

Nineteen Eighty-Four, George Orwell (Penguin 1950)

Ancient Wisdom, Modern World – Ethics for the New Millennium, Tenzin Gyatso His Holiness the Dalai Lama (Abacus 2000)

Beyond Lament, edited by Marguerite M Striar (Northwestern University Press, Illinois 1998)

Blessed Mother Teresa – Her Journey To Your Heart, T T Mundakel (Simon and Schuster UK, 2003)

Colour of Justice, The, transcripts of the Stephen Lawrence inquiry edited by Richard Norton-Taylor (Oberon Books, 1999)
Consciousness Explained, Daniel C Dennett (Penguin 1993)

Divided City – The Berlin Wall (Jaron Verlag GmbH, Berlin 2002)

Emmeline Pankhurst, Paula Bartley (Routledge 2002)

For A Dancer, Jackson Browne (on the album Late For the Sky, Elektra/Asylum Records 1974)

Hegel – A Very Short Introduction, Peter Singer (Oxford University Press 1983)

Imagine, John Lennon (EMI Records Ltd 2000)

Jerusalem in the Time of Jesus, Professor Joachim Jeremias (translated by F H and C H Cave, SCM Press Ltd 1969)

Lennon – the definitive biography, Ray Coleman (Pan Books 2000)

Let Me Take You Down, Jack Jones (Virgin Publishing 1993)

Orange for Farewells (The Connection at St Martin-in-the-Fields, 2002)

Return of the Prodigal Son, The, a story of homecoming, Henri J M Nouwen (Darton Longman and Todd 1994)

Smelling It Straight (The Connection at St Martin-in-the-Fields, 2001)

Spirit, Mike Scott (on the Waterboys' album 'This is the Sea', Ensign Records Ltd 1985)

Steve and Me, My friendship with Stephen Lawrence and the search for justice, Duwayne Brooks with Simon Hattenstone (Abacus 2003)

The Nation's Favourite Poems, The (BBC Worldwide Ltd, 1996)

INDEX OF SUBJECTS AND THEMES

ABOUT THE AUTHOR

Douglas Board was born in Hong Kong in 1957. He received degrees from Cambridge and Harvard, and worked in government and then in executive search, where he is deputy chairman of Saxton Bampfylde Hever plc. He is a trustee of the Diana, Princess of Wales Memorial Fund.

He has worshipped at St Martin-in-the-Fields Church in Trafalgar Square, London since 1979.